CHESS

ENDGAME CHALLENGES

ABOUT THE AUTHOR

Grandmaster Larry Evans, one of America's most celebrated chess authorities, is a 5-time USA champion and author of more than twenty chess books including *New Ideas in Chess*, *10 Most Common Chess Mistakes*, 200 *Chess Endgame Challenges*, and his collaboration on Bobby Fischer's classic, *My 60 Memorable Games*. He was a long-time contributor to *Chess Life*, and his syndicated chess column, "Evans on Chess," had appeared continuously for almost 40 years. Evans has beaten or drawn games against six world champions: Euwe, Karpov, Petrosian, Spassky, Smyslov, and Fischer, as well as dozens of the world's top players.

Evans first won the Marshall Club Championship at age fifteen and the New York State Championship at age sixteen. He won the USA Closed Championship five times (the first time in 1951, the last time in 1980—a remarkable span), the USA Open four times, the 1956 Canadian Open, and had numerous wins at many other opens including first place at an international tournament in Portugal in 1974. Evans represented the USA on eight Olympic teams (including the gold medal team in 1976) and served as captain in 1982. Evans was the youngest player to capture the nation's highest chess title at age nineteen, a record surpassed by Bobby Fischer at age fourteen. He is sometimes referred to as "The Dean of American Chess."

200 CHESS ENDGAME CHALLENGES

LARRY EVANS

5-TIME U.S. CHAMPION

CARDOZA PUBLISHING

Cardoza Publishing is the foremost gaming publisher in the world with a library of more than 200 up-to-date and easy-to-read books and strategies. These authoritative works are written by the top experts in their fields and with more than 10,000,000 books in print, represent the best-selling and most popular gaming books anywhere.

Formerly titled Chess Endgame Quiz

Library of Congress Catalog Card No: 2017960446
ISBN 13: 978-1-58042-359-5

Visit our web site (www.cardozabooks.com) or write us
for a full list of Cardoza books, advanced, and computer strategies.

CARDOZA PUBLISHING
P.O. Box 98115, Las Vegas, NV 89193
Phone (800)577-WINS
email: cardozabooks@aol.com
www.cardozabooks.com

TABLE OF CONTENTS

INTRODUCTION

This book is aimed at players who want to sharpen their endgame skills, and I have selected 200 instructive, elegant and challenging positions that are also fun to solve. The problems are divided into sections such as king and pawn endings, rook and pawn endings, queen endings, and minor piece endings, so that you can either concentrate on these areas for training and learning purposes, or simply to challenge yourself.

You are given three choices for each of the positions but only one of them is superior. What is the best move? It's up to you to figure it out!

THE IMPORTANCE OF THE ENDGAME

The *endgame* (or ending) is the final phase of a chess game. Mastering the basics is not only of immediate practical value, enabling us to squeeze out extra points from seemingly dry positions, but also of lasting value since the rules have been codified for centuries. These principles are timeless, often involving beautiful nuances exquisite timing, and even a touch of poetry.

The endgame is vastly neglected because so much analysis is lavished on wresting an advantage in the opening. To achieve success, however, we must study all aspects of the game and not succumb to the temptation of learning a few fashionable openings by rote.

There are no second chances in the endgame. Many players are weak here because they find it dull, or get tired, or lack practice. But it's no fun to throw away the fruit of your labor after hours of hard work. I'm still kicking myself for a simple win that I overlooked in 1966 (see diagram 45). "There is no remorse like the remorse of chess," said H. G. Wells. "No chess player sleeps well. You see with more than daylight clearness that it was the rook you should have moved, not the knight."

Renowned artist Marcel Duchamp, who virtually gave up painting for chess, illustrated a book on distant opposition in kings and pawn endings, because he was beguiled by their geometric patterns. "His obsession with the game intensified as he grew older," noted *The Oxford Companion to Chess*. "Of his marriage in 1927 [his friend] Man Ray noted: "Duchamp spent most of the one week they lived together studying chess problem and his bride, in desperate retaliation, got up one night when he was asleep and glued the chess pieces to the board. They were divorced three months later."

Needless to day, I'm not trying to destroy anyone's marriage.

THE KING HAS TWO FACES

"The king is a fighting piece. Use it!"
—Wilhelm Steinitz

"Uneasy lies the head that wears a crown."
—Shakespeare

In the opening, nothing is more important that safeguarding the king by castling early (usually within the first dozen moves). Leaving him in the center too long is the leading cause of disaster, even among top players. But when there is little danger of getting mated both kings can rush to the center with impunity. The victor is often he who gets there "fustest with the mostest."

"My king likes to go for a stroll."
—Wilhelm Steinitz

Not many players dare to heed this admonition because it's too risky to expose the king to attack in the opening or middle game. During most of the game the king must bide his time, cringing behind his own forces for safety while the foot soldiers take the hits. "Only at the end can the king use his power," said playwright Samuel Becket, who knew a thing of two about third acts.

Indeed, the king has two faces. Freudians might diagnose him as schizophrenic—sometimes weak, sometimes strong—definitely a split personality. The contrast is striking between the king's role in the opening and ending.

> "Having sat out the whole game behind the pawn bastions in his own camp, the king now becomes an active attacking piece and tries to participate in the struggle with all its might. It preys on the opponent's pieces and is often the first to force its way into the enemy camp." —Yuri Averbach

ELEMENTARY, MY DEAR MATES

The object is to mate the enemy king, but don't count on it happening very soon unless your opponent is extremely careless. How many times can you get away with the elementary Fool's Mate: (1 e4 e5 2Bc4 Bc5 3Qh5 Nc6?? 4Qxf7)? If neither side makes a serious mistake, then a war of attrition is likely.

> "Most games are won in the middle game, but you must know something about the endgame. You will need to know how to win if you are a pawn up or have some other small advantage, You also want to know how to defend if you get a bad endgame, and how to set about saving the draw." —David Hooper

After showing students how the pieces move and the meaning of checkmate, I turn to rudimentary endings: how to mate with queen, then rook, then two bishops, and finally bishop and knight against a long king (the most difficult). This helps us grasp the power of various pieces and how they work together.

But most people are anxious to get started right away and tend to think, "Why can't we just play a game and worry about all that stuff later?"

The answer: "Because you're not ready yet."

What good is it to gain material early in a game if we can't exploit it at the end of a game? We must learn the alphabet before we can write or read music before composing a symphony. Creativity is any discipline comes only after we master the fundamentals.

WHEN DOES THE END BEGIN?

I'm frequently asked whether grandmasters agree on when the endgame begins. The answer is no. It's sometimes a matter of opinion. There is no clearcut dividing line between the middle game and the endgame. This is determined by two factors: a reduction in material and no real danger of mounting a direct attack on either king.

As a rule of thumb, the endgame begins when the queens are gone. Take the Berlin Defense to the Ruy Lopez that was rehabilitated by Vladimir Kramnik against Garry Kasparov in their 2000 title match: 1 e4 e5 2 Nf3 Nc6 3 Bb5 Nf6 4 00 Nxe4 5 d4 Nd6 6 Bxc6 dxc6 7 dxe5 Nf5 8 Qxd8+ Kxd8.

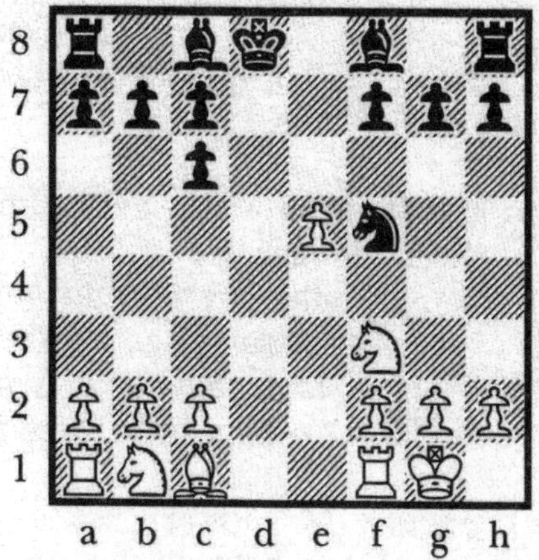

Position after 8...Kxd8

You could call this a middle game or an endgame even though most of the men are still on the board. Is it the beginning of the end or the end of the beginning?

> "In many ways, the complexity of chess is exemplified in the endgame, since there are fewer pieces to rely upon and increased mobility and terrain for those that remain. The opportunities for deeper and more exact calculations are therefore that much greater, and the demands on precision and imagination abound."—Frank Brady

GRAMMAR OF THE ENDGAME

There are four essential tools of the trade:

1. Opposition
2. Stalemate
3. Zugzwang
4. Triangulation

This is the grammar of the endgame. There is no need to memorize specific positions. Once we understand these basic concepts, we are well on our way to solving knotty problems that are likely to arise over the board in our own games.

1. ***Opposition*** is a situation where the two opposing kings stand on the same rank, file or diagonal and are separated from each other by an odd number of squares. It is usually beneficial to keep the opposition to prevent the other king from penetrating. Whoever is on move is said to "lose the opposition." See page 18.

2. ***Stalemate*** is a type of draw that occurs when a player whose turn it is to move is *not* in check but has no legal move available. It is the single most important defensive resource for a player who faces almost certain defeat and plays a prominent role in many of these endgame studies.

3. ***Zugzwang*** (German for forced to move) describes a predicament when a player is compelled to make a move under duress when he would prefer to pass. You are in zugzwang when any move you make will seriously weaken your position, though the opposition poses no concrete threat.

> "The right of moving in chess is at the same time an obligation. In by far most instances the right to move is of great value, but there are cases where to move is disadvantageous. The laws of chess do not permit a free choice: you have to move whether you like it or not." —Emanuel Lasker

Having the move is almost always a blessing, though in rare situations it can be a curse. This example is from a Fischer-Taimanov match game in 1971.

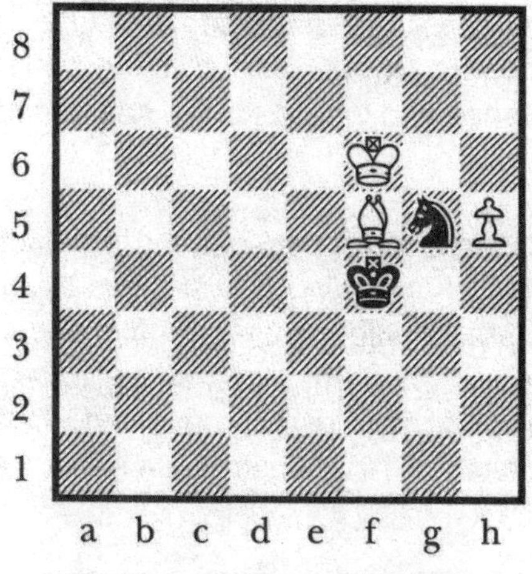

Black to move – and lose

Taimanov would like to pass but he can't and resigned after 1…Nf3 2 h6 Ng5 3 Kg6 Nf3 (Zugzwang: Black could draw if he never had to make another move!) 4 h7 Ne5+ 5 Kf6 and the pawn can't be stopped. See diagram 184.

Whoever moves loses a pawn and the game!

Trebuchet, French for balance, is a unique kind of zugzwang where whoever is on move must alter the delicate balance and lose, as in the solution to diagram 181.

4. ***Triangulation*** is a rare maneuver by which a piece (usually a king—see diagram 3) takes two moves to reach a square it could have reached in one, in effect losing a move. The term probably originated because a triangular pattern is usually involved. This famous study composed in 1922 illustrates a curious queen triangulation.

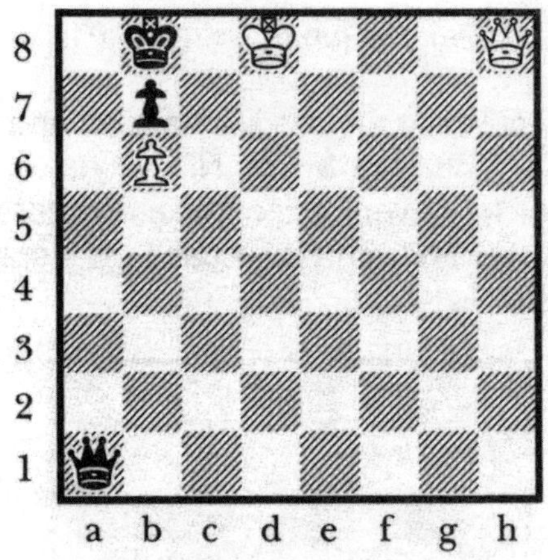

White to play and win

Black is hoping to draw after 1 Qxa1 stalemate. But if his king were on a8 instead of b8, then his queen could be captured *with check*. If 1. Qe8 (threatening Kd7 mate) then Qa4! once again offers the queen as bait. (See the solution in diagram 111.)

> "The unique importance of the endgame is that after it there is nothing more. After a bad opening there is hope for the middle game. After a bad

middle game there is hope for the endgame. But once you are in the endgame the moment of truth has arrived. The game will end here in a win, draw, or loss." —Edmar Mednis

WHY THIS BOOK?

The following letter from a reader inspired me to write this book:

> "I would never deep six my tattered copy of Reuben Fine's *Basic Chess Endings* which has steered me through some tricky shoals using his fine (if sometimes flawed) navigation. But since I bought it 25 years ago I, like many others, have tried to add, delete, tape, paste, blot out, and otherwise keep up with more recent analysis pointed out by careful readers in your *Chess Life* column. Is there a worthwhile and trustworthy compilation of corrections to this classic? If not, is there a comparable one-volume you'd recommend to supplement Dr. Fine's opus?"

Alas, there is no one volume in English that can compare with the nearly 600 densely packed pages of Fine's brilliantly organized *Basic Chess Endings*. It served as a beacon for my generation and was the one book that I always took to international tournament.

I hope this multiple-choice quiz is a painless way to master basic theory without wading through reams of esoteric analysis. Each diagram offers three plausible alternatives. Your task is to find the best solution. At the end of the series perhaps you will discover a new respect for the endgame as well as increased skill in every phase of the game.

This book is divided into four sections, each consisting of 50 diagrams. The first deals with king and pawn endings arising after all the other combatants have lost their lives in the course of battle. These are disarmingly simply but contain hidden resources. The second deals with rook and paw endings, which are the most likely to occur in practical play. A rook, like a king, acquires real power in an open battlefield. The third examines queen and pawn endings, which often arise after a pawn has been promoted to a new queen. The fourth focuses on minor piece endings after the major pieces (queens and rooks) are gone.

These 200 brainteasers either occurred in or were inspired by actual games. Many famous composers of pure endgame studies were weak players working in splendid isolation who rarely competed in tournaments. Their creations aim at instructing as well as astonishing the solver with an extraordinary twist.

> "The principle aim of the artistic endgame is to please. The means? All are allowed; one alone is ruled out—the tedious! The aim of the composer is not just what the solver will find at the end of the road, but the beauty along the trail." —Andre Cheron

There's an old saying that trifles make perfection, but perfection is no trifle. Nowhere in chess is this more true than in the endgame. I envy readers who have the good fortune to savor these delights for the first time.

—*Larry Evans*

KING & PAWN ENDINGS

Basic Opposition
Berlin 1904

White to Play and Draw

(a) Ke3 (b) Ke4 (c) Kf4

Composed by Sackmann

White to Play and Win

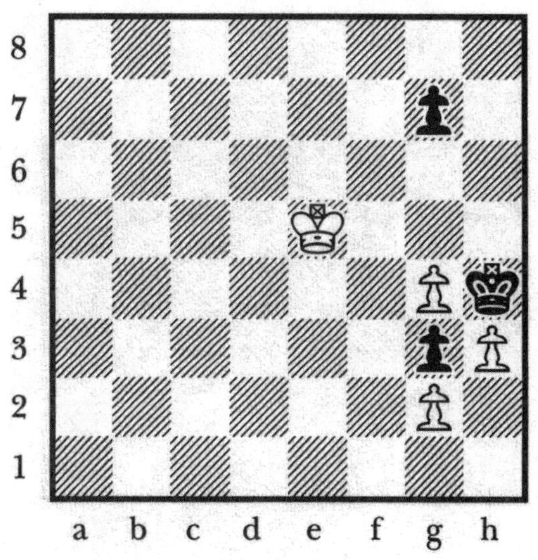

(a) Kf4 (b) Kf5 (c) g5

Composed by Walker

White to Play and Win

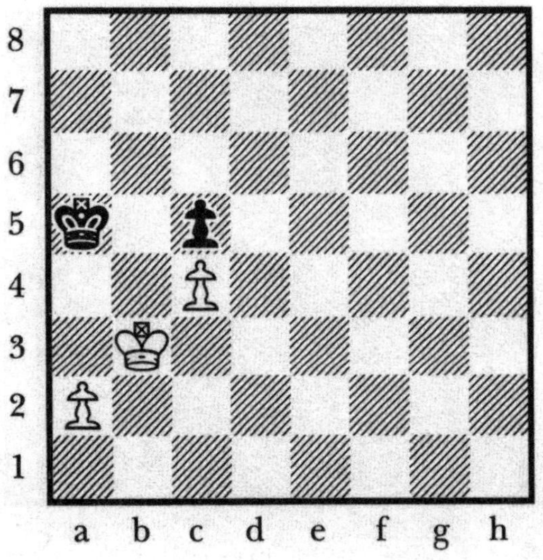

(a) Ka3 (b) Kc3 (c) Kc2

Composed by Rinck

White to Play and Win

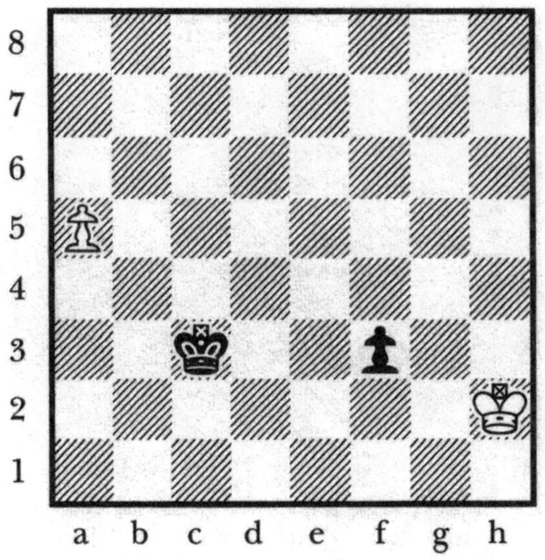

(a) Kg1 (b) Kg3 (c) a6

Schlage vs. Ahues
Berlin 1921

White to Play and Win

(a) Kd7 (b) Kd5 (c) Kd6

Composed by Moravec

White to Play and Win

(a) b4 (b) Kb1 (c) Ka2

Composed by Horwitz

White to Play and Win

(a) Kd3 (b) Kc3 (c) Kb1

Composed by Dobias

White to Play and Win

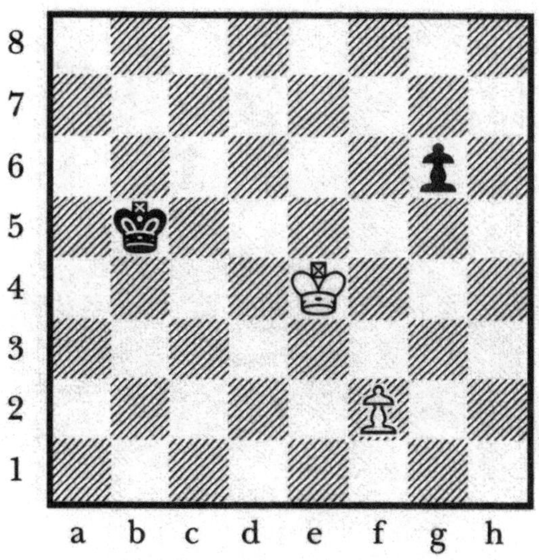

(a) Kd4 (b) Kd5 (c) Ke5

Composed by Duras

White to Play and Win

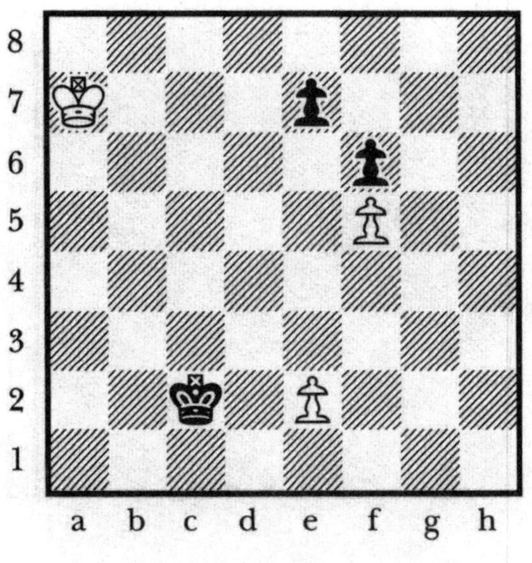

(a) Kb8 (b) Kb7 (c) Kb6

Composed by Grigoriev

White to Play and Draw

(a) Kd5 (b) Kf5 (c) Kf6

Composed by Fahrni

White to Play and Win

(a) g6 (b) h6 (c) f6

Chigorin vs. Tarrasch
Ostend 1905

White to Play and Draw

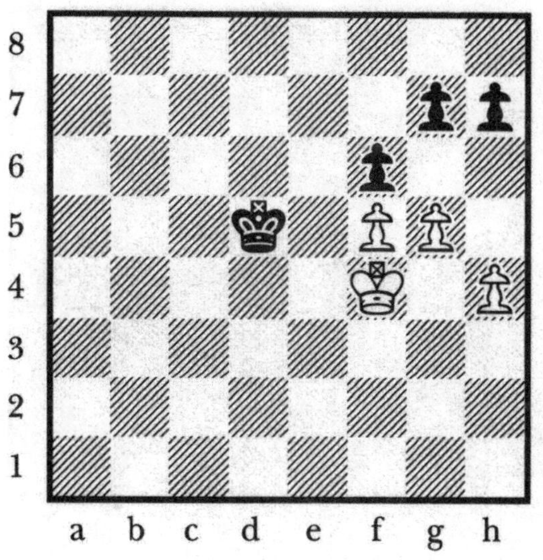

(a) Kg4 (b) g6 (b) h5

Radoicic vs. Cvetkovic
Yugoslavia 1999

White to Play and Draw

(a) Kg2 (b) c5 (c) f3

Composed by Grigoriev

White to Play and Win

(a) Ka6 (b) Kc5 (c) b3

Composed by Grigoriev

White to Play and Win

(a) b6 (b) Kb4 (c) Ka6

16

Composed by Herbstmann

White to Play and Win

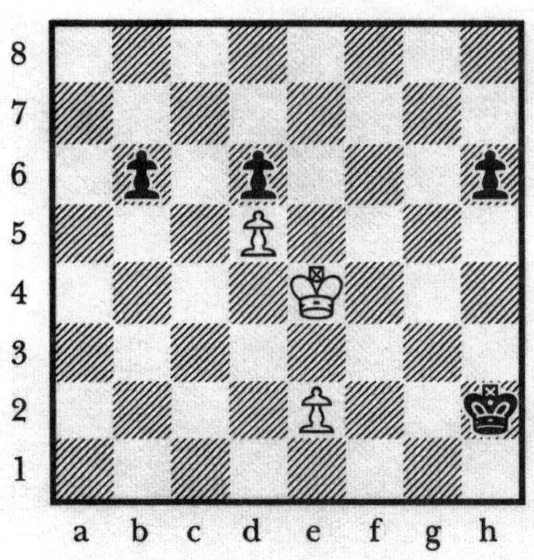

(a) Kf3 (b) Kf5 (c) Kd4

Riga Society vs. Polytechnic School
Riga 1892

White to Play and Draw

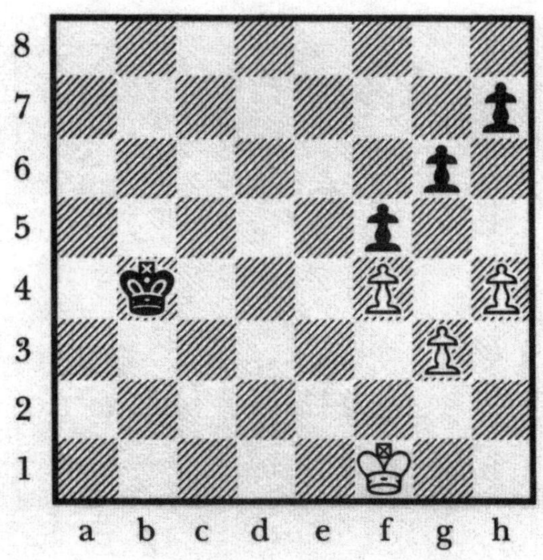

(a) Kg2 (b) Ke2 (b) h5

Composed by Pospisil

White to Play and Win

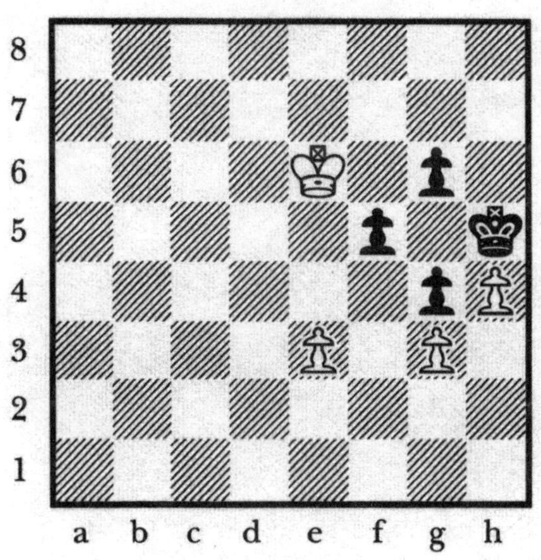

(a) Kf6 (b) Kf7 (c) Ke7

Composed by Rothlander

White to Play and Win

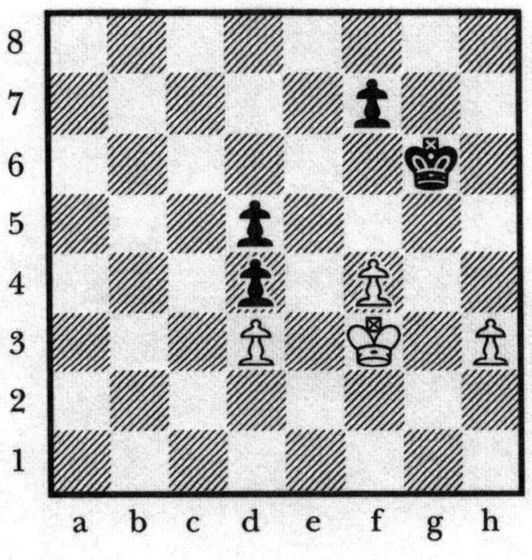

(a) Kg4 (b) f5+ (c) h4

Ed. Lasker vs. Molle

Berlin 1904

White to Play and Win

(a) f4 (b) f6 (c) g5

Mason vs. Englisch
London 1883

White to Play and Win

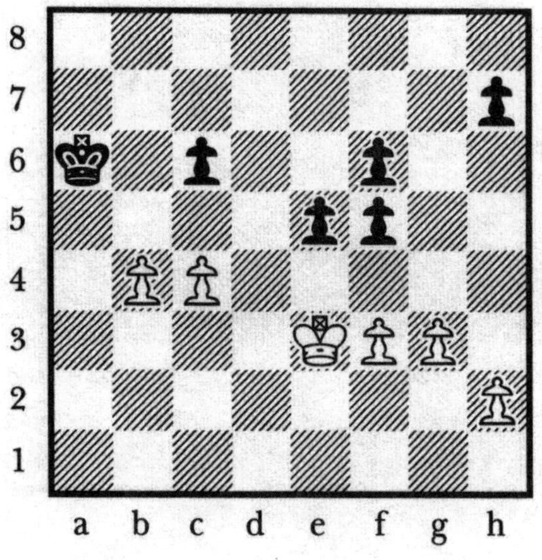

(a) g4 (b) f4 (c) h3

Alekhine vs. Yates
Hamburg 1910

White to Play and Win

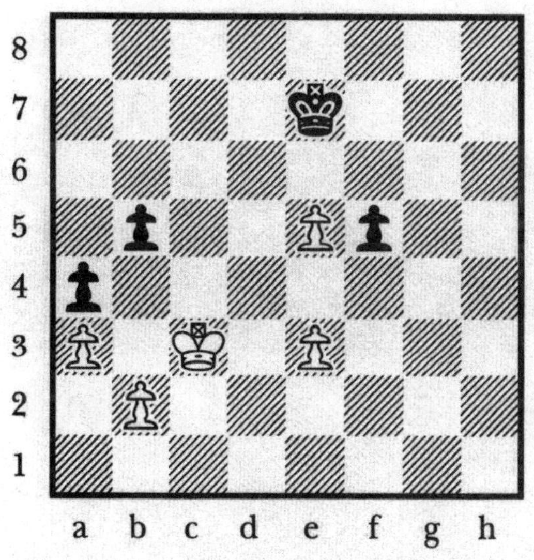

(a) Kd3 (b) Kd4 (c) Kb4

Thomas vs. Maroczy
Nice 1930

White to Play and Win

(a) g4 (b) h4 (c) Ke4

Composed by Grigoriev

White to Play and Win

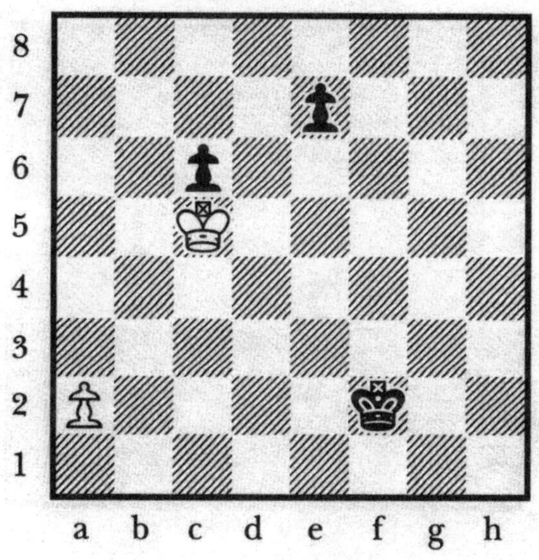

(a) a4 (b) Kxc6 (c) Kd4

Composed by Labourdonnais

Black to Play and Draw

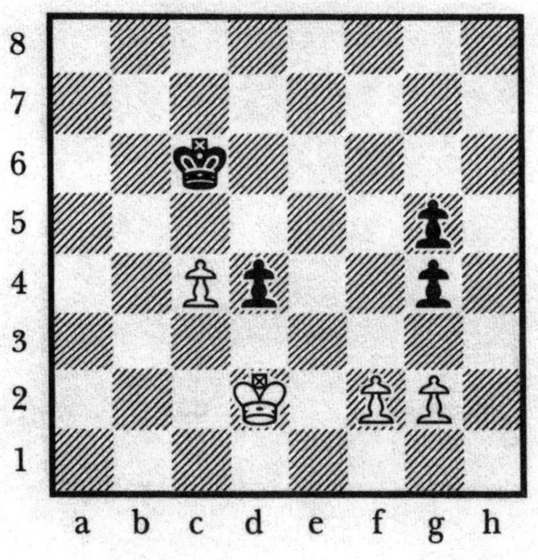

(a) Kc5 (b) Kd6 (c) g3

Shirov vs. Timman
Wijk aan Zee 1996

Black to Play and Draw

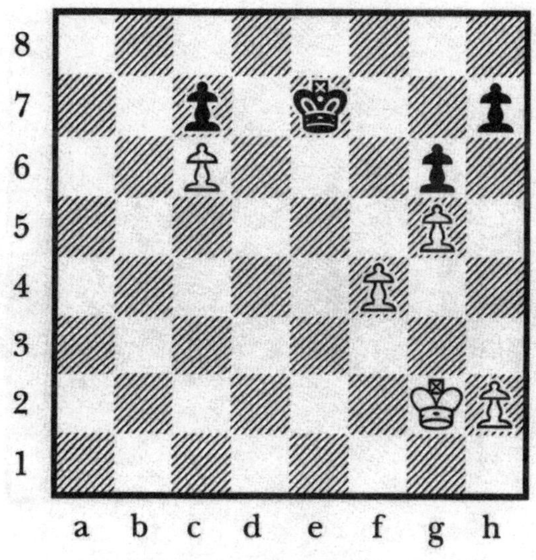

(a) Kf7 (b) Kd6 (c) Ke6

Teichmann vs. Blackburne
Berlin 1897

Black to Play and Win

(a) h4 (b) c5 (c) g4

Ilyukhin vs. Novopolsky
USSR 1954

Black to Play and Win

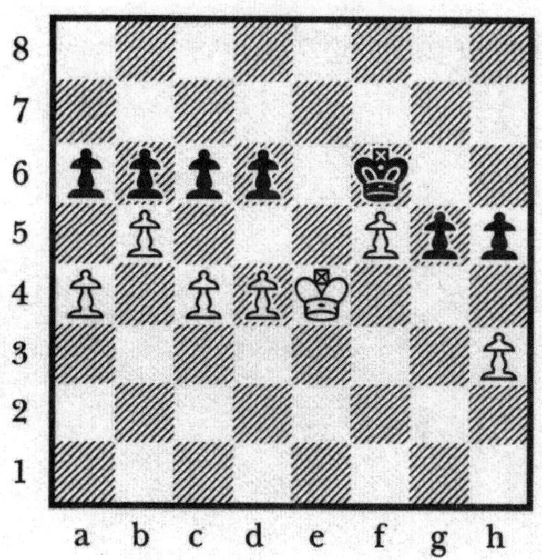

(a) axb5 (b) cxb5 (c) d5+

Tarrasch vs. Schiffers
Nuremburg 1896

Black to Play and Draw

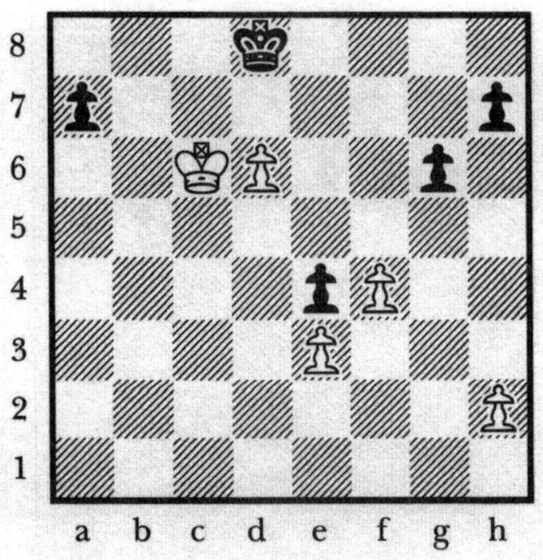

(a) h6 (b) Kc8 (c) a5

Taimanov vs. Botvinnik
Moscow 1953

Black to Play and Win

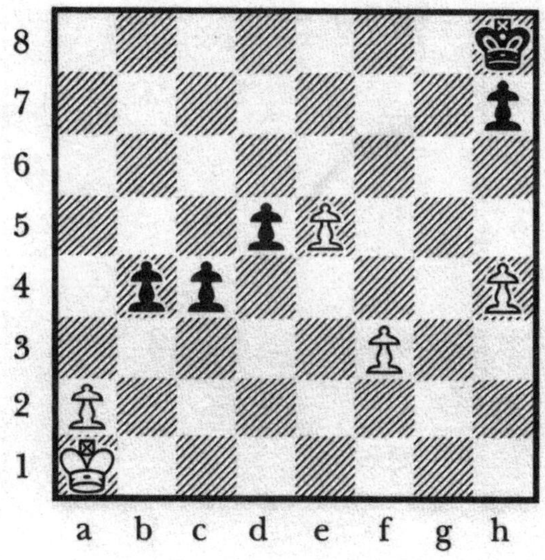

(a) d4 (b) c3 (c) Kg7

Euwe vs. Alekhine
34th match game 1935

Black to Play and Win

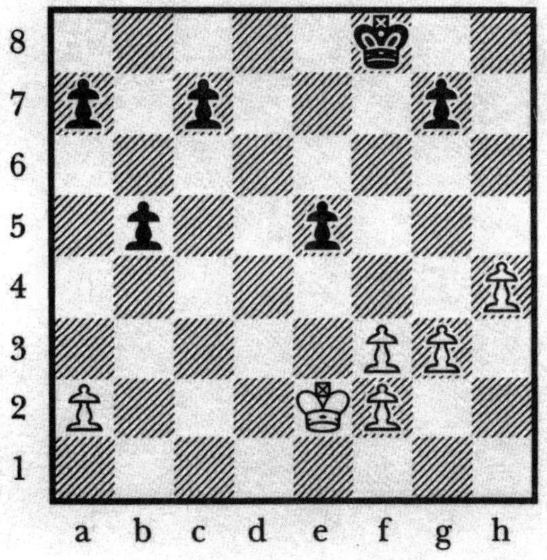

(a) c5 (b) a5 (c) Ke7

Muller vs. Rhode
postal game 1897

Black to Play and Win

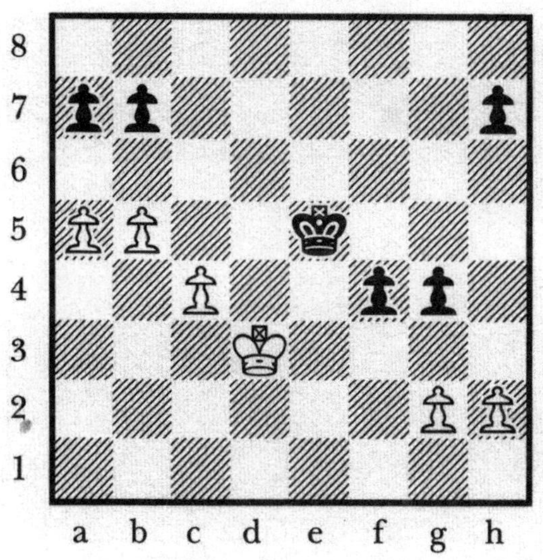

(a) f3 (b) h5 (c) b6

Stahlberg vs. Tartakower
offhand game 1934

Black to Play and Win

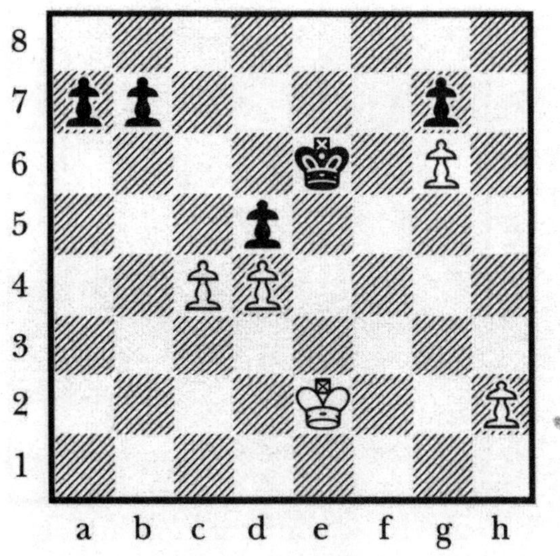

(a) dxc4 (b) a5 (c) Kf5

Krutyansky vs. Zagorovsky
Moscow 1952

Black to Play and Win

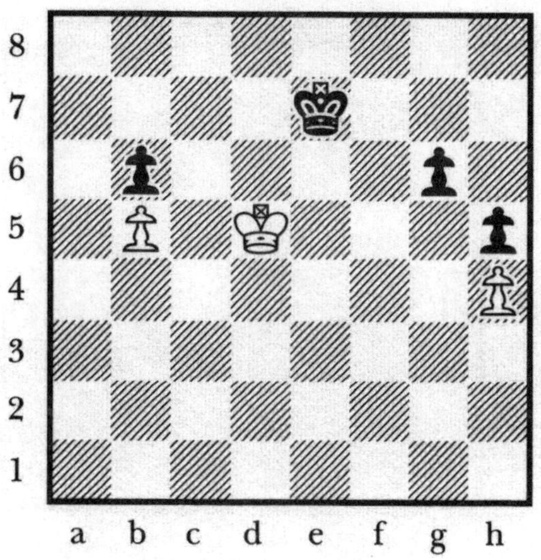

(a) Kd7 (b) Kf6 (c) Kf7

Chekhover vs. Bondarevsky
Leningrad 1938

Black to Play and Draw

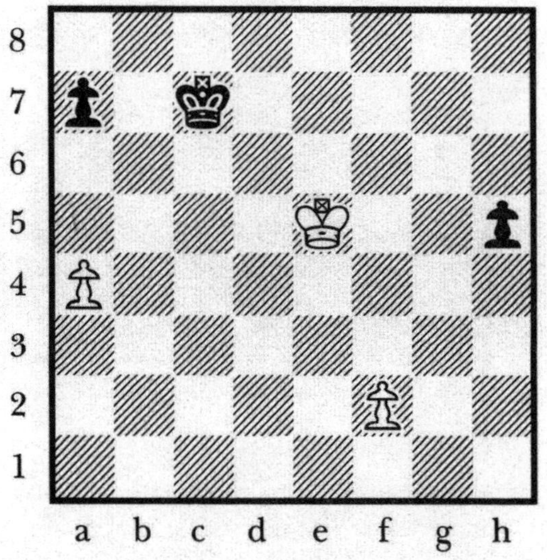

(a) a5 (b) Kc6 (b) (c) a6

Grob vs. Nimzovich
Zurich 1934

Black to Play and Draw

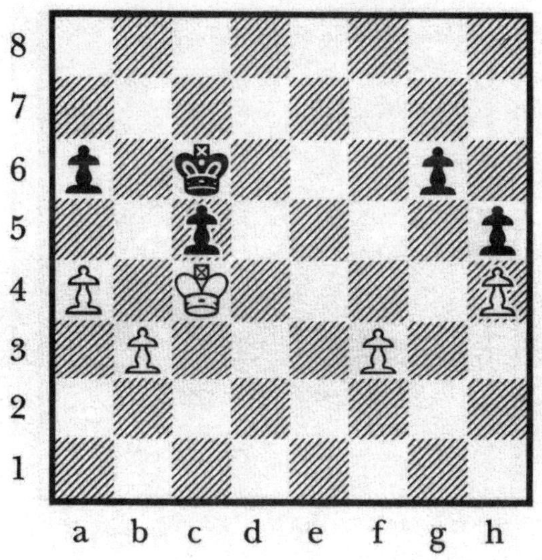

(a) Kb6 (b) Kd6 (c) Kd7

Randviir vs. Keres
Parnu 1947

Black to Play and Win

(a) h6 (b) Kb5 (c) Kb6

Euwe vs. Pirc
6th match game 1949

Black to Play and Draw

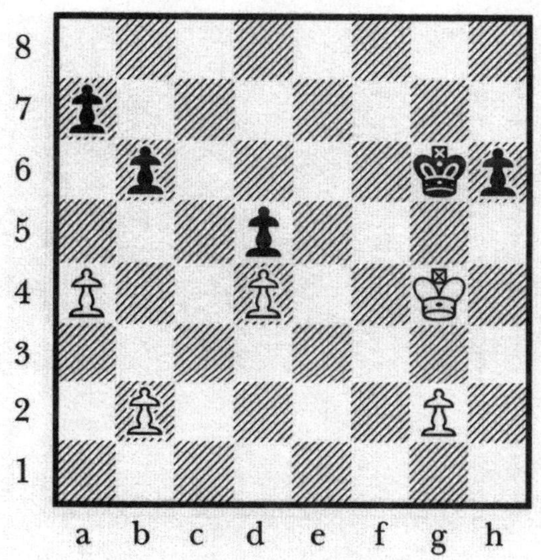

(a) a5 (b) a6 (c) Kf6

Havasi vs. Stahlberg
Budapest 1934

Black to Play and Win

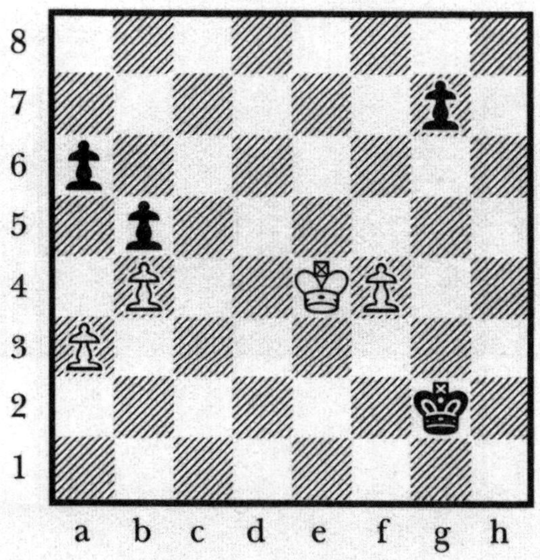

(a) Kf2 (b) Kg3 (c) g6

Composed by Bahr

Black to Play and Draw

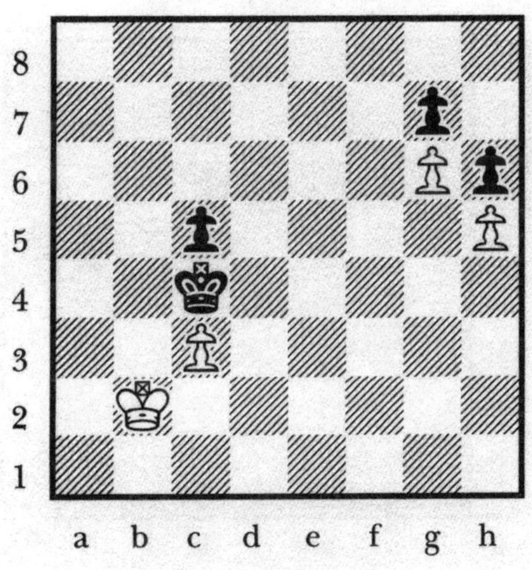

(a) Kb5 (b) Kd5 (c) Kd3

Composed by Grigoriev

Black to Play and Draw

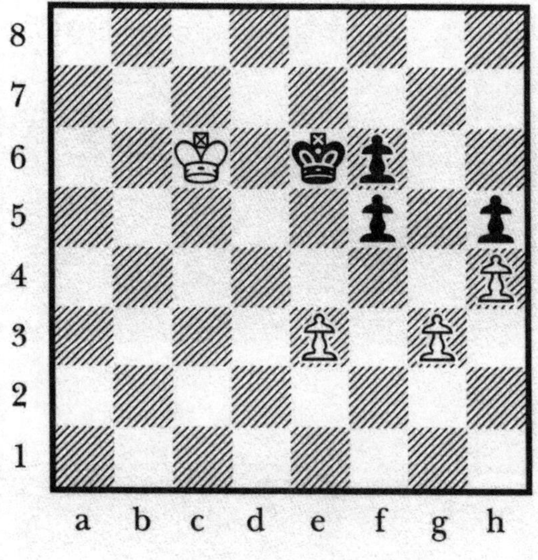

(a) Ke5 (b) Ke7 (c) f4

Composed by Zhigis

White to Play and Draw

(a) Kg4 (b) Kf4 (c) Ke4

Composed by Duras

White to Play and Win

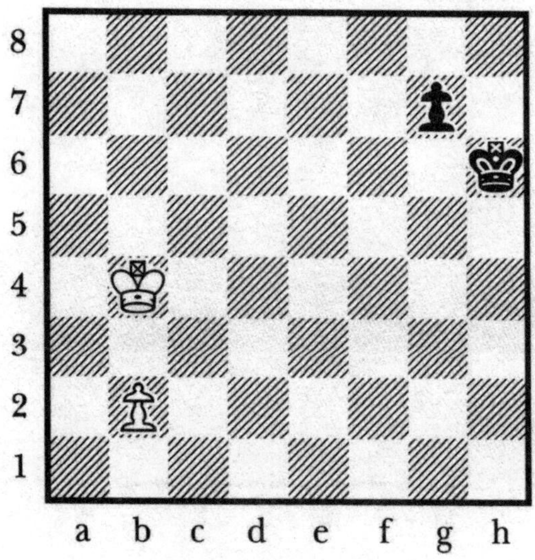

(a) Kc5 (b) Kc3 (c) Kc4

Evans vs. McCormick
Lone Pine 1971

White to Play and Draw

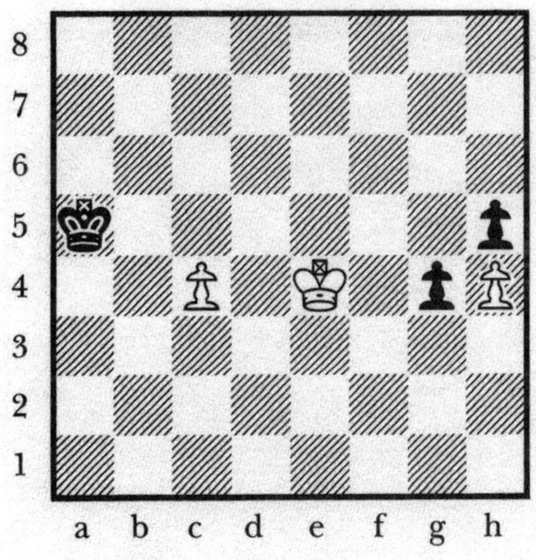

(a) Kd5 (b) c5 (c) Kd3

Evans vs. Benko
Las Vegas 1966

White to Play and Win

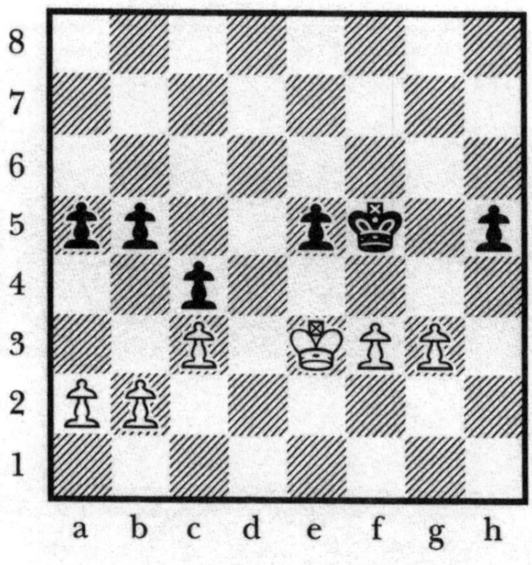

(a) a3 (b) g4+ (c) Kf2

Composed by Grigoriev

White to Play and Win

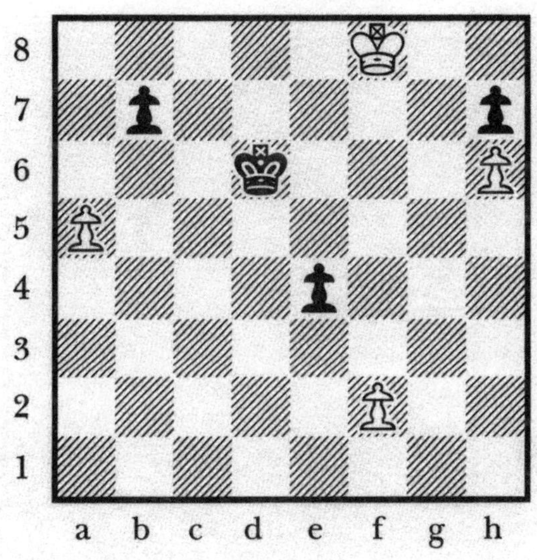

(a) Kf7 (b) Kg7 (c) Ke8

Composed by Grigoriev

White to Play and Draw

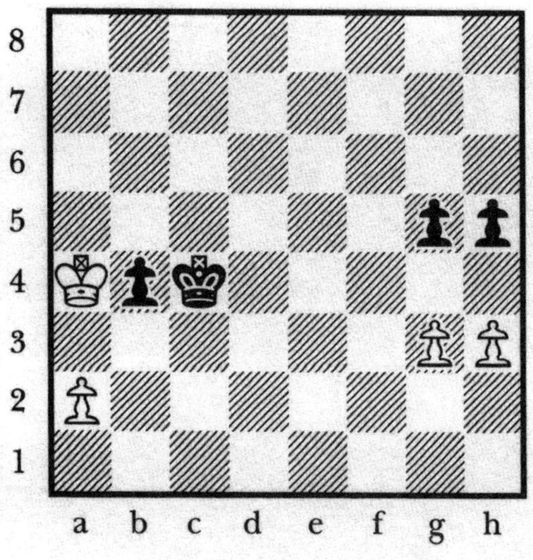

(a) g4 (b) h4 (c) Ka5

Composed by Grigoriev

White to Play and Win

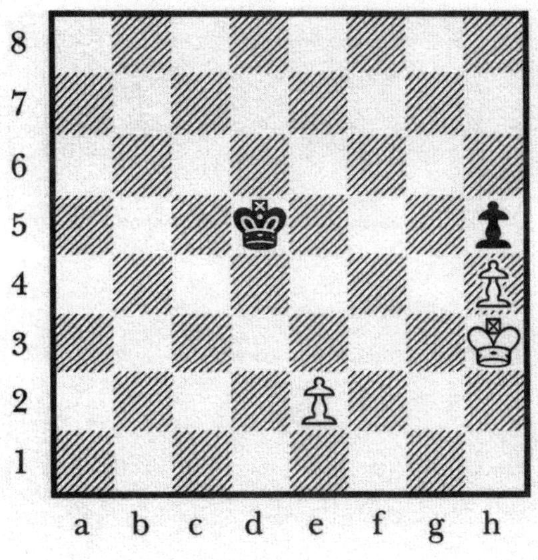

(a) Kg3 (b) Kg2 (c) Kh2

Composed by Halberstadt

White to Play and Draw

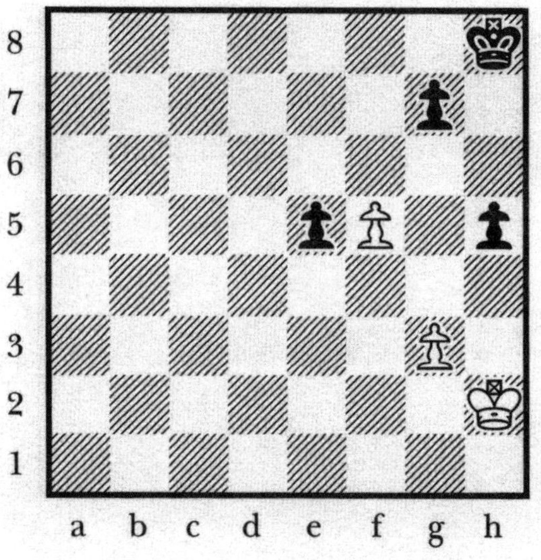

(a) Kg2 (b) g4 (c) Kh3

Wade vs. Korchnoi
Buenos Aires 1960

White to Play and Win

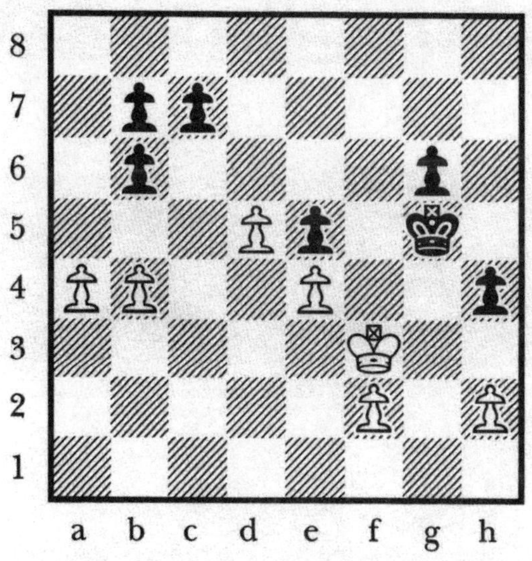

(a) b5 (b) h3 (c) a5

ROOK & PAWN ENDINGS

The Lucena Position

White to Play and Win

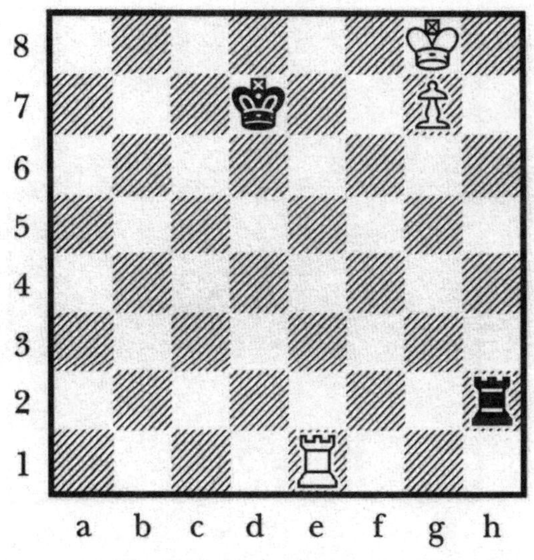

(a) Kf7 (b) Re4 (c) Re5

The Philidor Position

White to Play and Draw

(a) Ra3 (b) Rf7+ (c) Kf1

Philidor's Analysis

White to Play and Draw

(a) Rf1 (b) Kd1 (c) Kf1

Composed by Kling & Horwitz

White to Play and Win

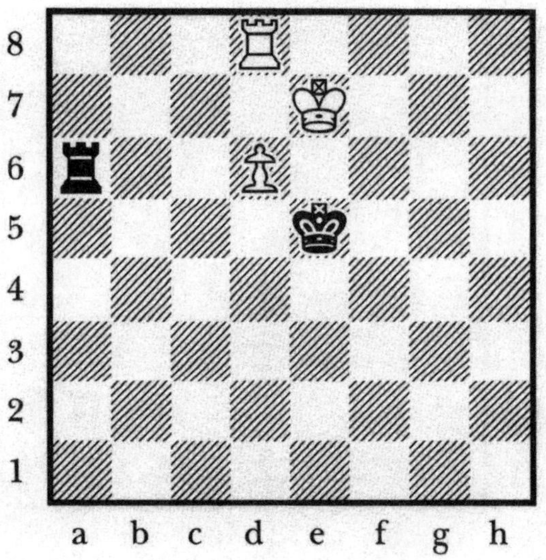

(a) d7 (b) Rh8 (c) Rg8

Potter vs. Fenton
England 1895

White to Play and Win

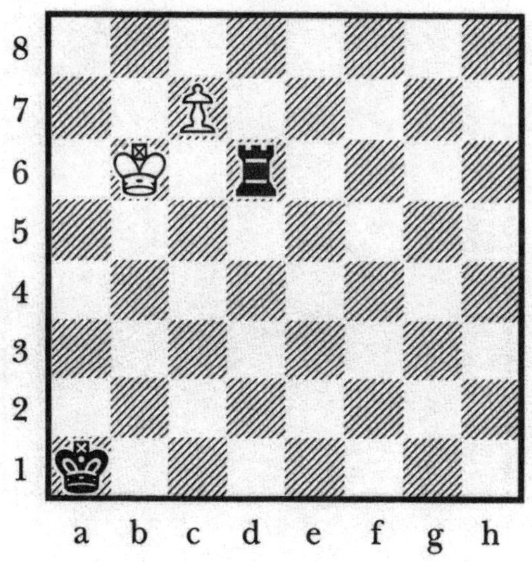

(a) Kc5 (b) Kb5 (c) Kb7

Composed by Selesniev

White to Play and Win

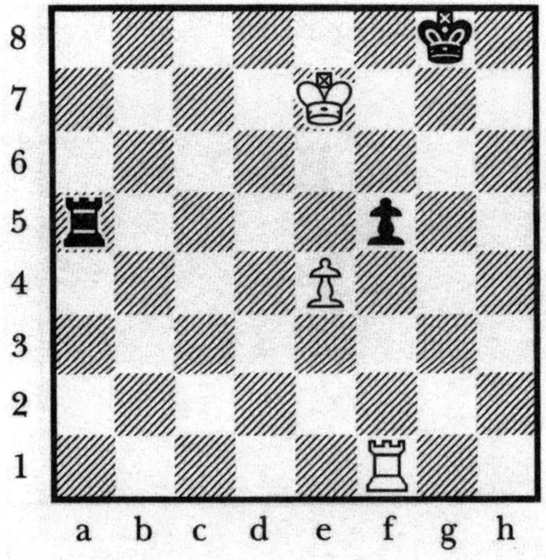

(a) exf5 (b) Rg1+ (c) Rxf5

Kochiev vs. Smyslov
Lvov 1978

White to Play and Draw

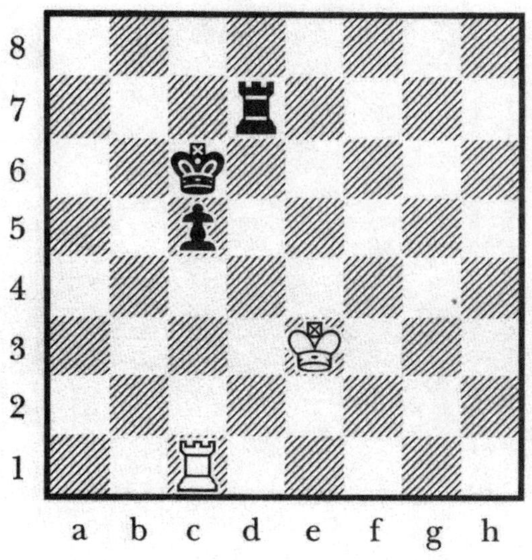

(a) Ke4 (b Ke2 (c) Rc2

Composed by Keres

White to Play and Win

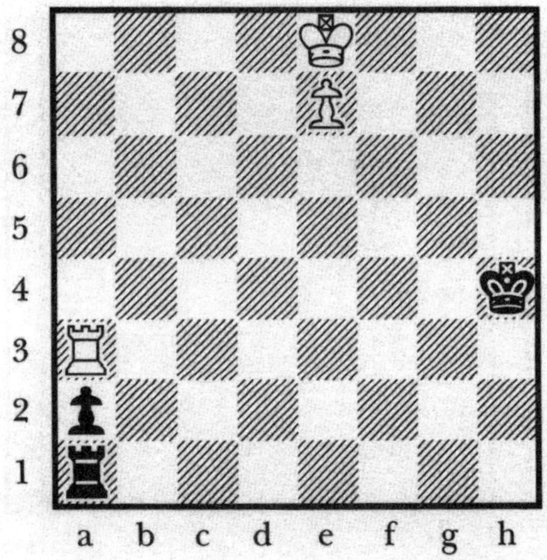

(a) Kf7 (b) Kd7 (c) Ra5

Composed by Em. Lasker

White to Play and Win

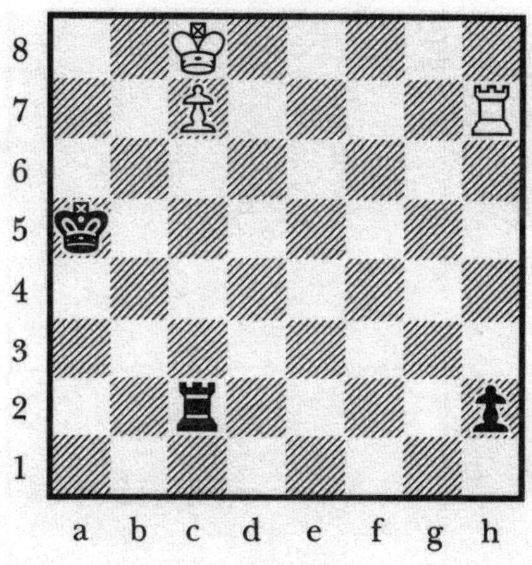

(a) Rh5+ (b) Kb7 (c) Kd8

Composed by Grigoriev

White to Play and Win

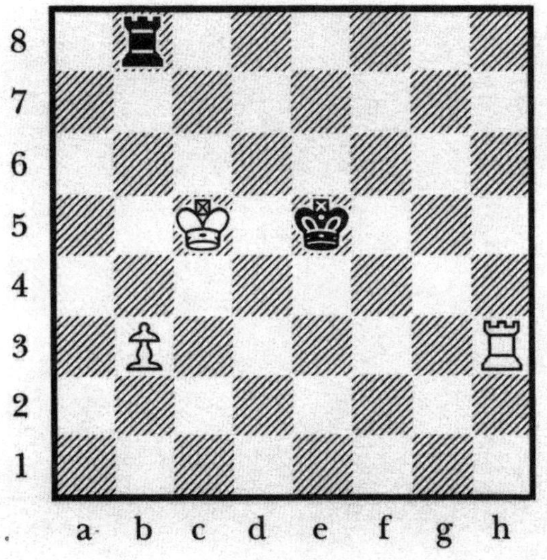

(a) b4 (b) Rh5+ (c) Rd3

Mestrovic vs. Griffiths
Hastings 1971/2

White to Play and Draw

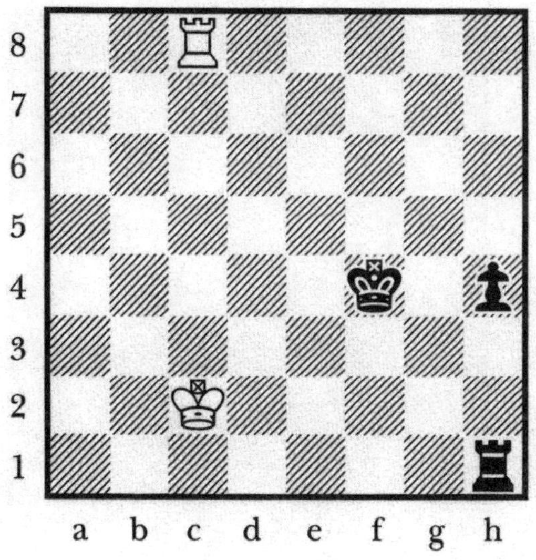

(a) Kd2 (b) Rh8 (c) Rf8+

Shirov vs. Kramnik
Belgrade 1999

White to Play and Win

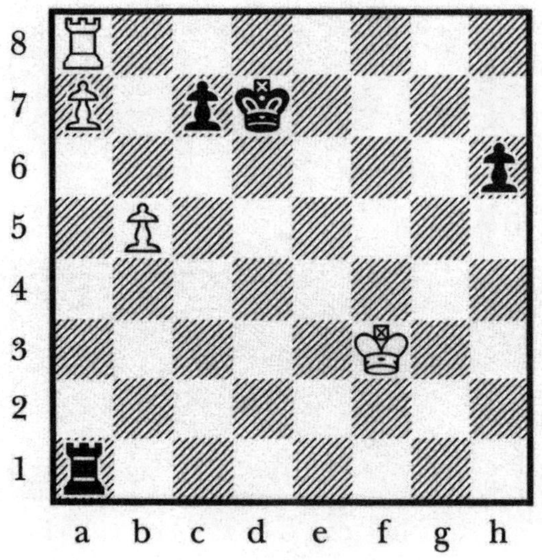

(a) b6 (b) Rh8 (c) Ke4

Adelman vs. Mote
Chicago 1998

White to Play and Win

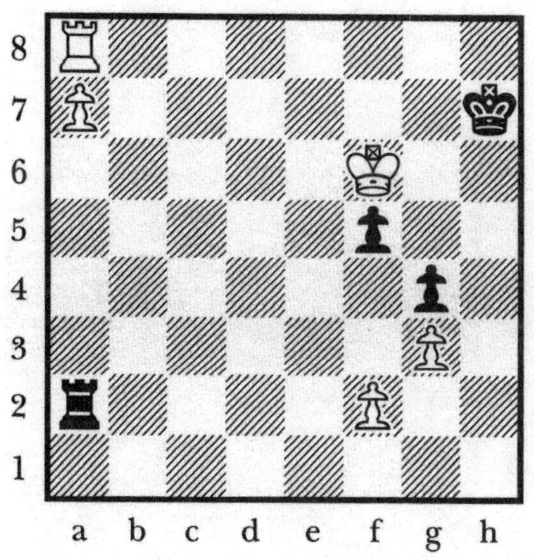

(a) Kxf5 (b) Kg5 (c) Rf8

Geller vs. Fischer
Mallorca 1970

White to Play and Draw

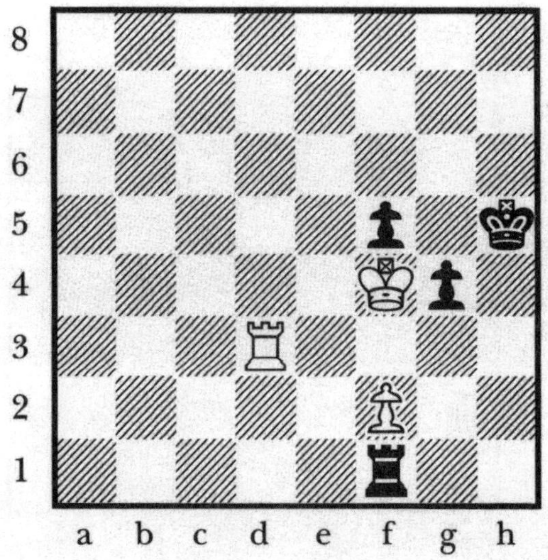

(a) Rd2 (b) f3 (c) Kg3

Composed by Selesniev

White to Play and Win

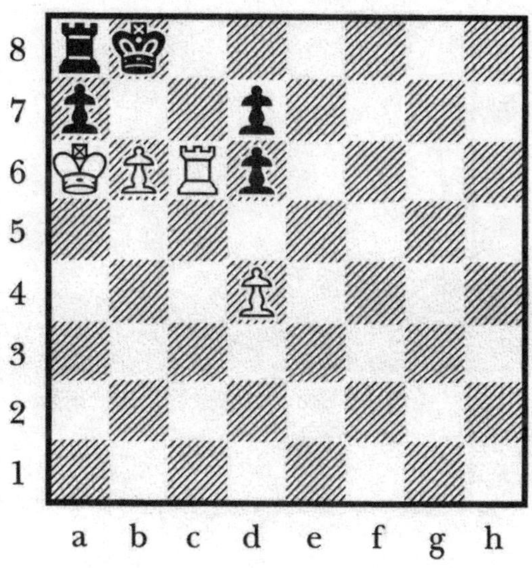

(a) Rc8+ (b) Rxd6 (c) Rc7

Composed by Selesniev

White to Play and Win

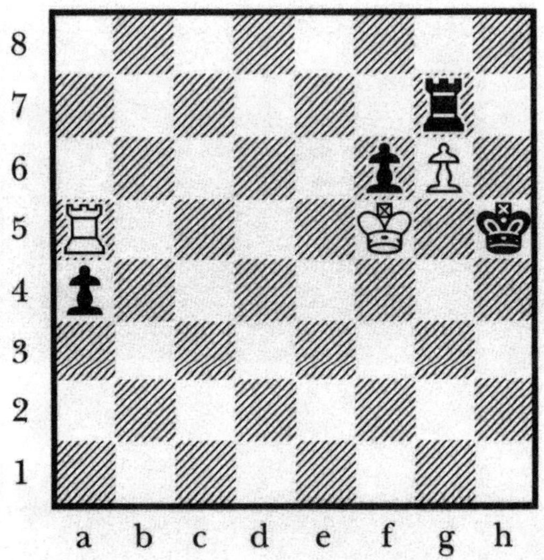

(a) Rxa4 (b) Kxf6+ (c) Ra8

Composed by Prokes

White to Play and Win

(a) Rf1 (b) Rg1 (c) Kd2

After Tarrasch vs. Janowski
Ostend 1907

White to Play and Win

(a) f7 (b) Ke5 (c) g7

Composed by Reti

White to Play and Win

(a) Rh4 (b) Rd2 (c) Rd1

Plater vs. Evans
Helsinki 1952

White to Play and Draw

(a) f7 (b) Kg7 (c) Kf7

Composed by Reti

White to Play and Draw

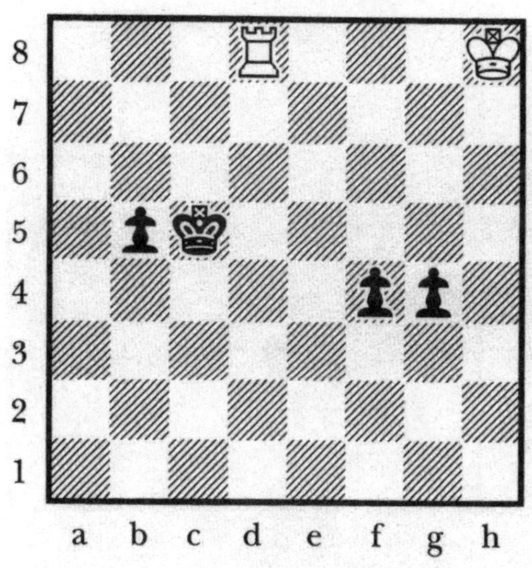

(a) Rc8+ (b) Rg8 (c) Rf8

Gligoric vs. Fuller
Hastings 1968/9

White to Play and Win

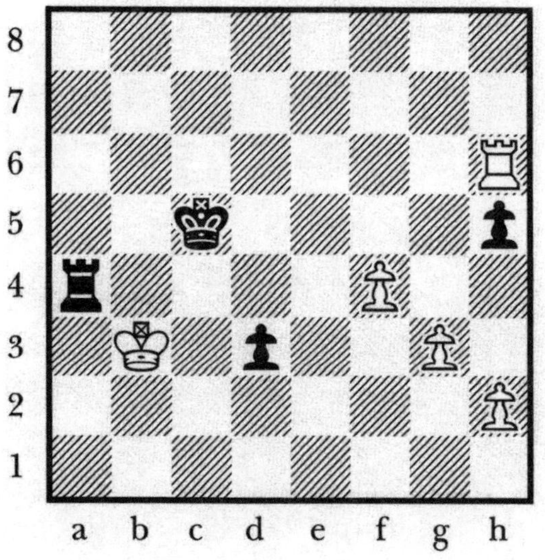

(a) Rxh5+ (b) Kc3 (c) Rh8

Composed by Troitzky

White to Play and Win

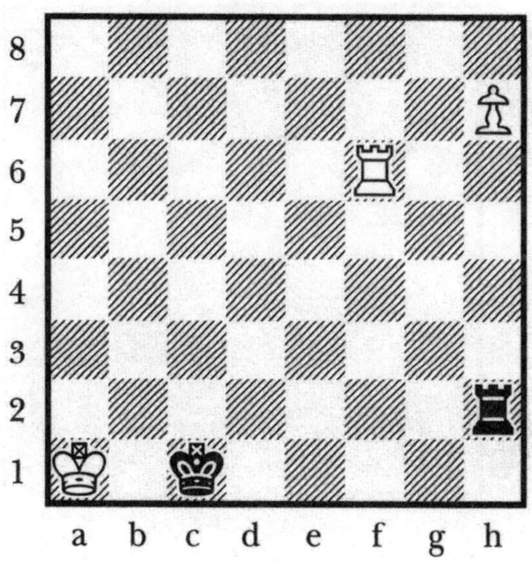

(a) Rc6+ (b) Rf1+ (c) Rf7

Maroczy vs. Tarrasch
San Sebastian 1911

White to Play and Win

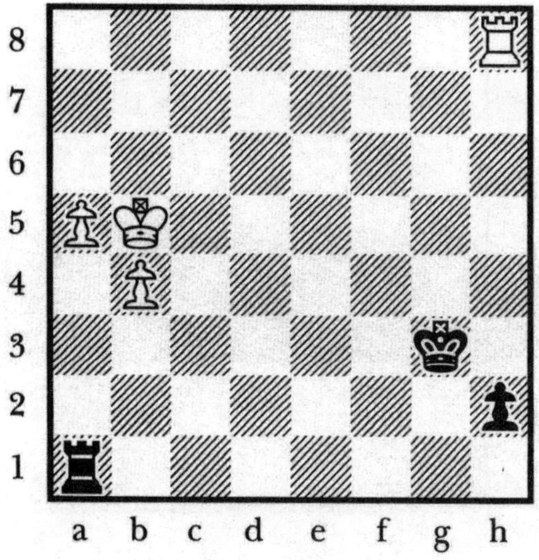

(a) Kc6 (b) Rxh2 (c) a6

Composed by Kling & Horwitz

White to Play and Win

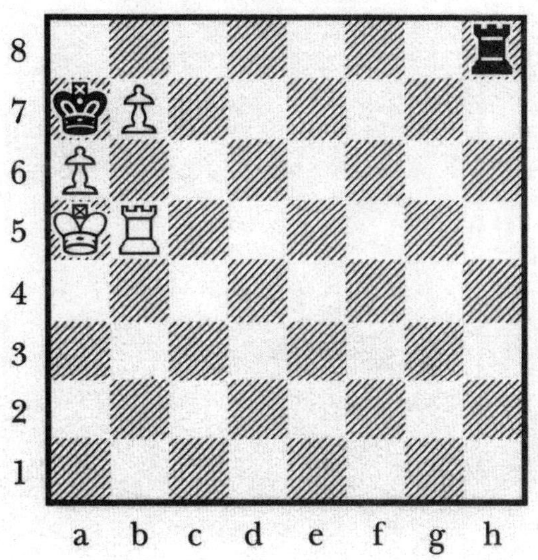

(a) Rb6 (b) Rc5 (c) Kb4

Composed by Kissling

White to Play and Win

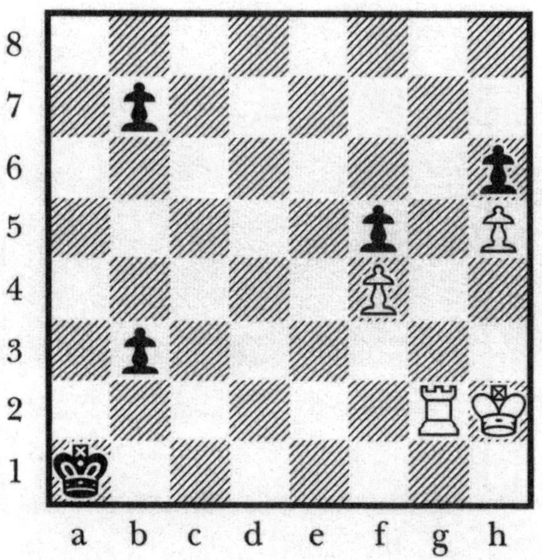

(a) Rg7 (b) Rg5 (c) Rg1+

Gufeld vs. Gulko
USSR 1985

White to Play and Draw

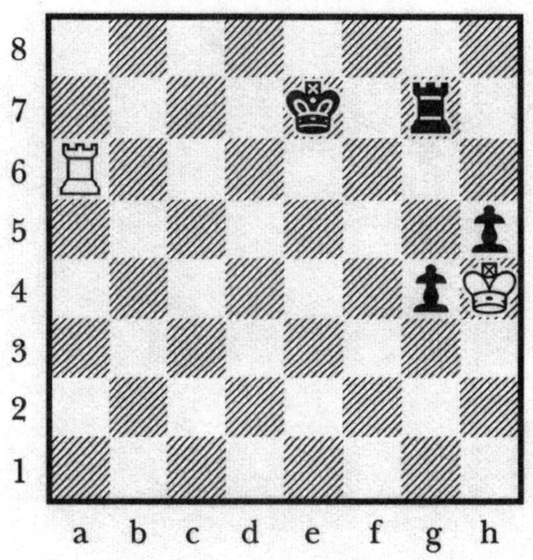

(a) Ra7+ (b) Rh6 (c) Kxh5

Alatortsev vs. Chekhover
USSR 1937

White to Play and Win

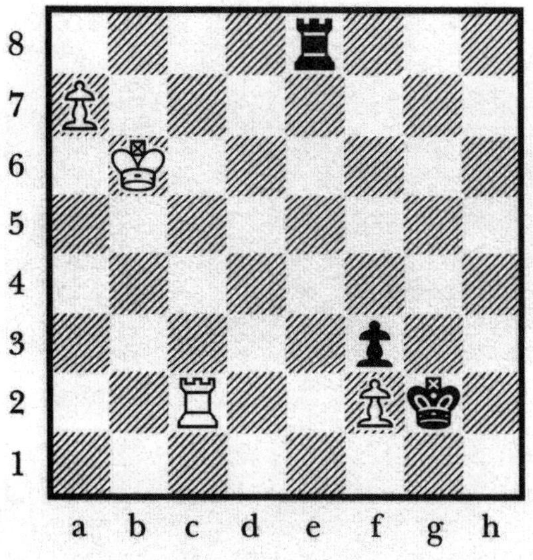

(a) Kb7 (b) Kc7 (c) Ra2

Acers vs. Hisper
New Orleans 1995

White to Play and Draw

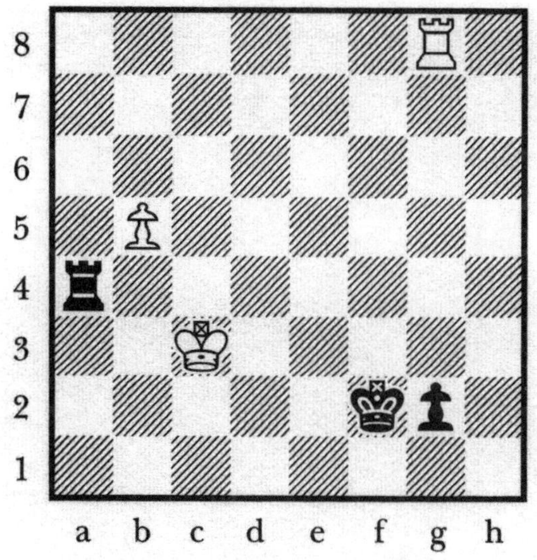

(a) b6 (b) Kb3 (c) Rf8+

Cohn vs. Hummel
Reno 1995

White to Play and Win

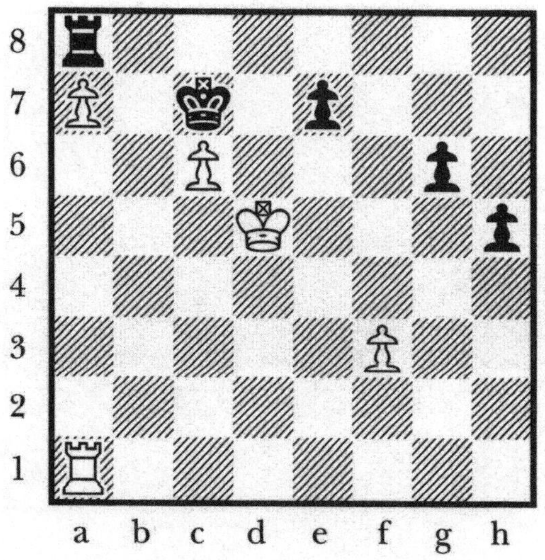

(a) Kc5 (b) Re1 (c) f4

Evans vs. Opsahl
Dubrovnik 1950

White to Play and Win

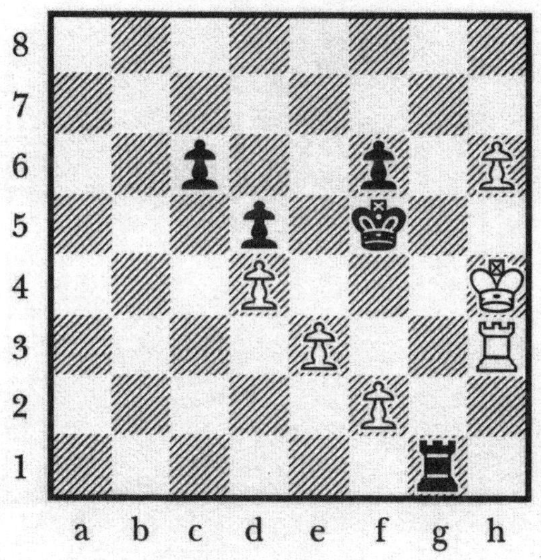

(a) h7 (b) Rf3+ (c) Rh2

Composed by Benko

White to Play and Win

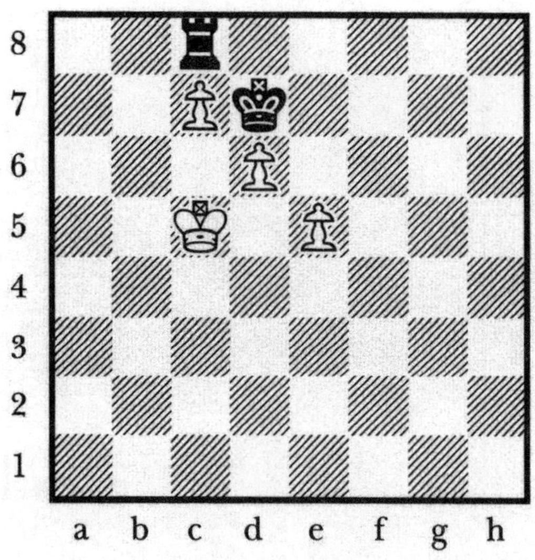

(a) e6+ (b) Kd5 (c) Kb6

Composed by Gurdenidze

White to Play and Win

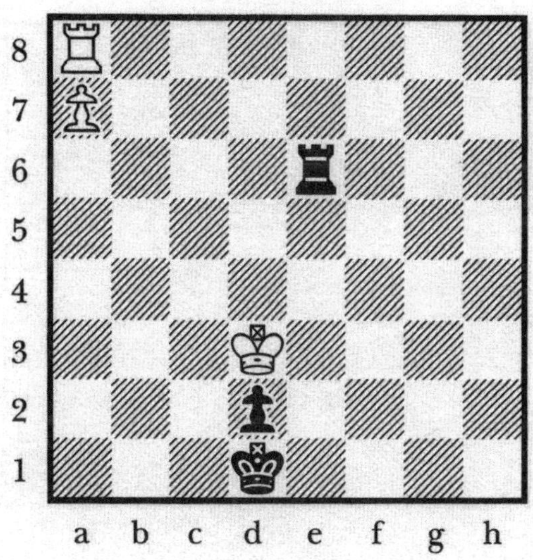

(a) Rd8 (b) Rb8 (c) Rh8

Stripunsky vs. Epishin
Philadelpha 1998

White to Play and Win

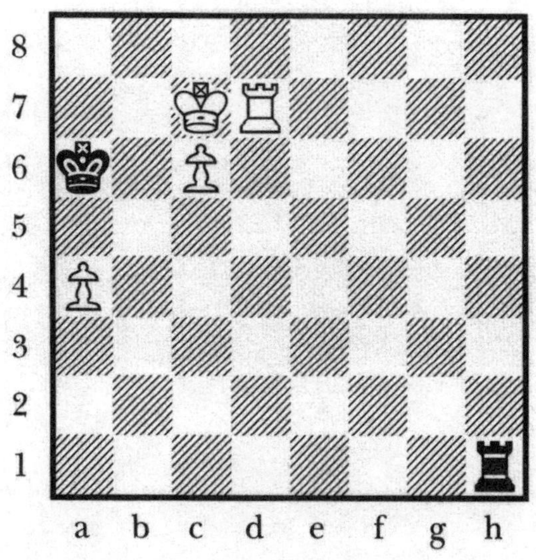

(a) a5 (b) Kc8 (c) Rd8

Composed by Kasparian

Black to Play and Draw

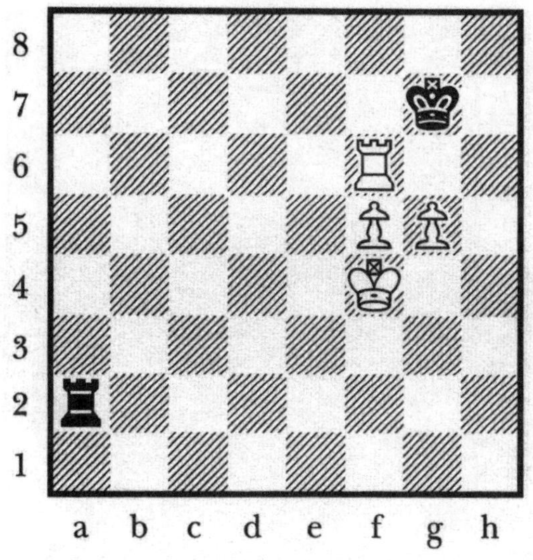

(a) Ra1 (b) Ra4+ (c) Rf2+

Composed by Seyburth

Black to Play and Draw

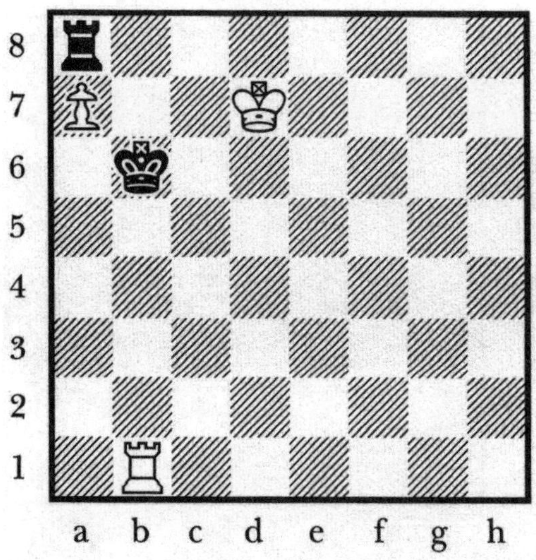

(a) Kxa7 (b) Ka6 (c) Kc5

Composed by Cheron

Black to Play and Draw

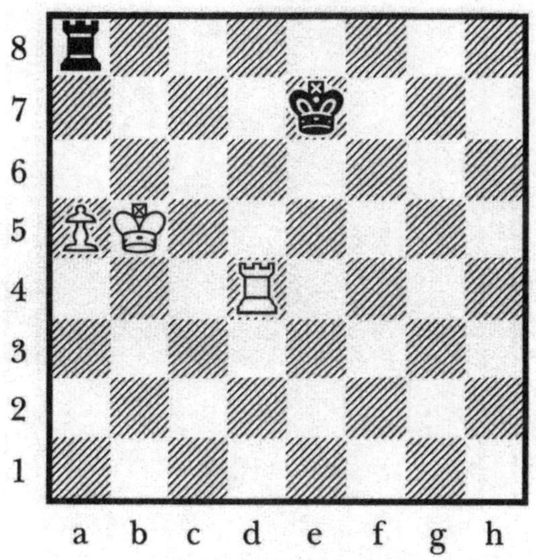

(a) Rd8 (b) Rb8+ (c) Rh8

Composed by Tarrasch

Black to Play and Draw

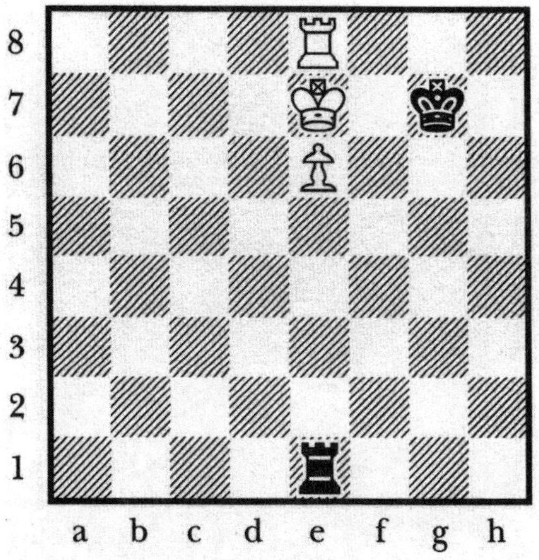

(a) Ra1 (b) Rb1 (c) Re2

Westerinen vs. Bobotsov
Venice 1971

Black to Play and Draw

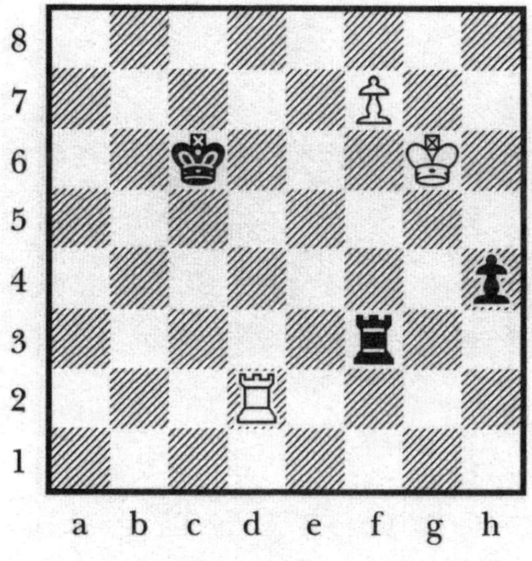

(a) h3 (b) Kc7 (c) Rg3+

Alekhine vs. Bogoljubow
19th match game 1929

Black to Play and Draw

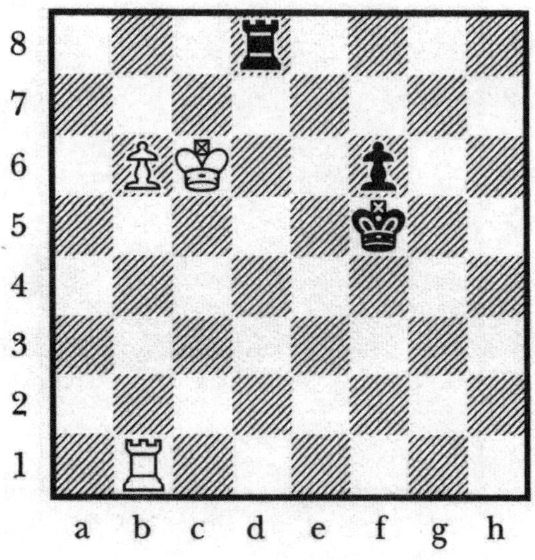

(a) Kg4 (b) Ke4 (c) Ke5

Alekhine vs. Bogoljubow
8th match game 1934

Black to Play and Win

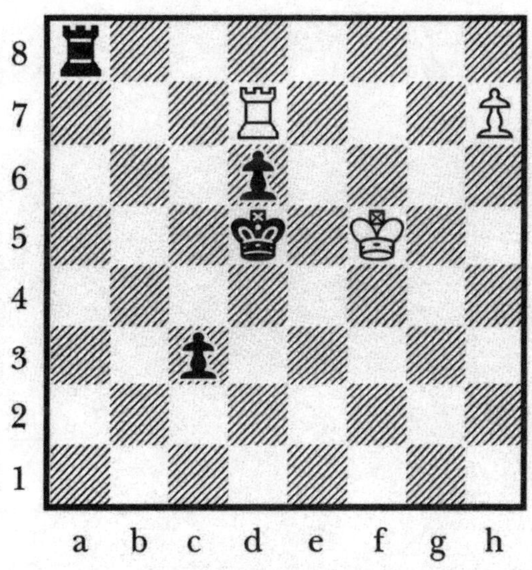

(a) Rc8 (b) Rh8 (c) Kc6

Reshevsky vs. Alekhine
AVRO 1938

Black to Play and Draw

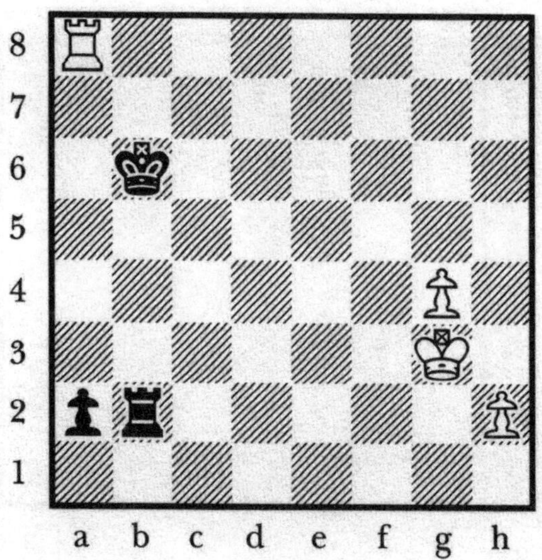

(a) Kb5 (b) Kb7 (c) Kc5

Keres vs. Mikenas
Estonia 1937

Black to Play and Draw

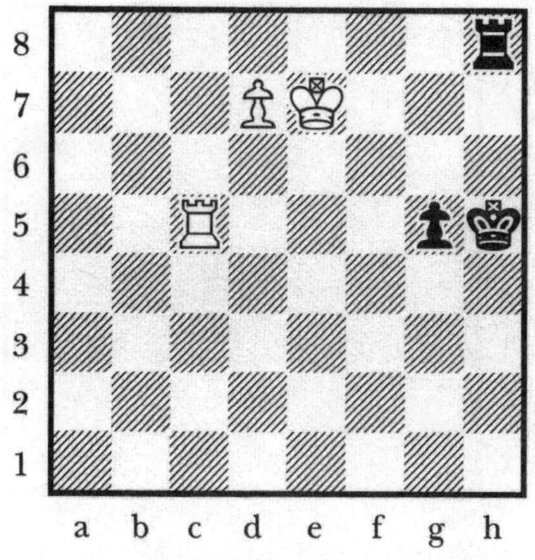

(a) Rh7+ (b) Kg4 (c) Kh4

Taimanov vs. Larsen
Mallorca 1970

Black to Play and Draw

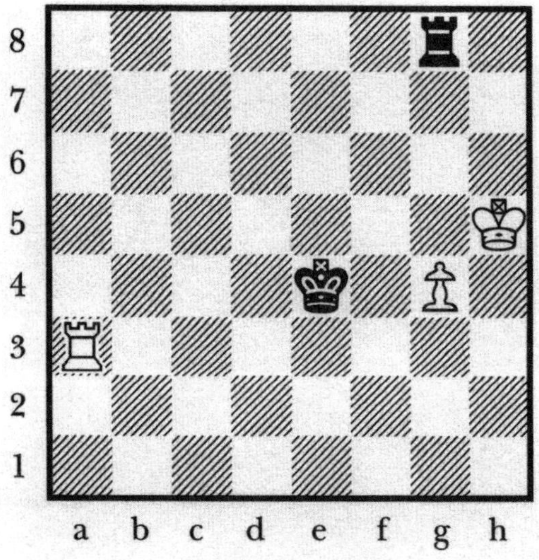

(a) Kf4 (b) Ke5 (c) Rh8+

Tarrasch vs. Chigorin
9th Match Game 1893

Black to Play and Draw

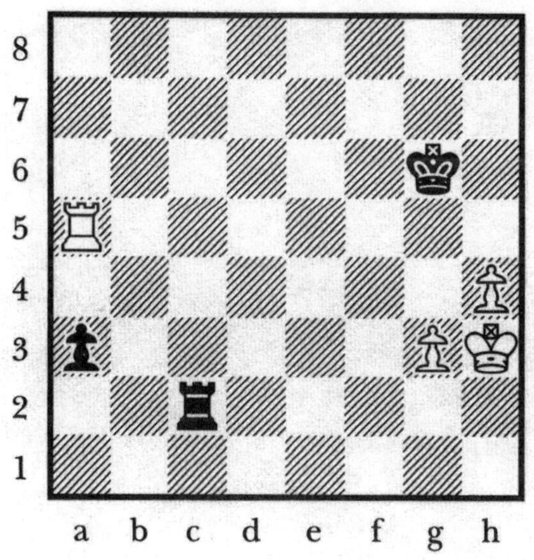

(a) Rc3 (b) Ra2 (c) a2

Kramnik vs. Topalov
Las Vegas 1999

Black to Play and Draw

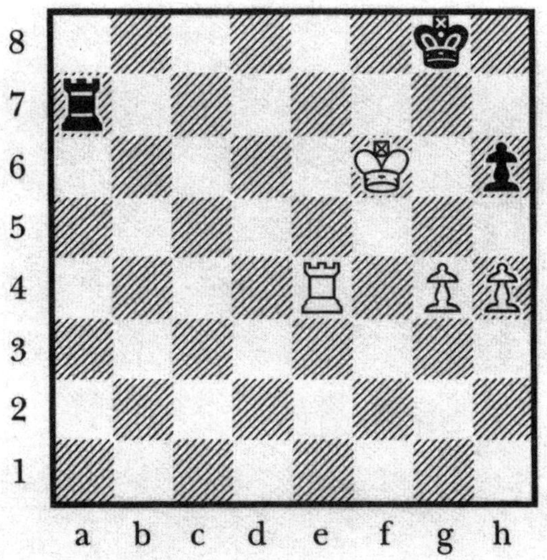

(a) Rg7 (b) Kh7 (c) Ra6+

Leko vs. Markowski
Polanica Zdroj 1998

Black to Play and Draw

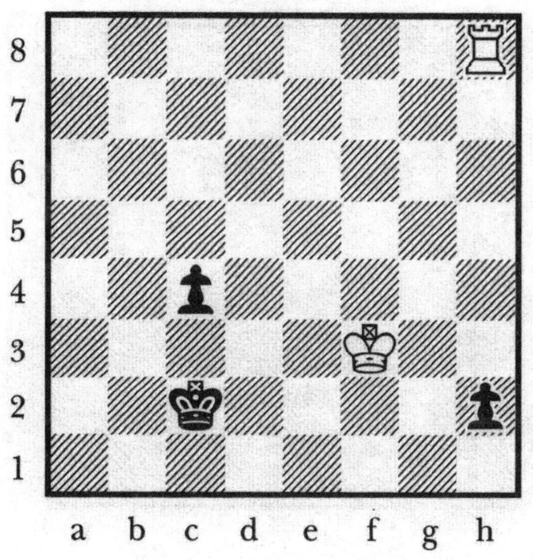

(a) Kd3 (b) Kd1 (c) c3

Gligoric vs. Smyslov
Moscow 1947

Black to Play and Draw

(a) Ra8 (b) Ra7+ (c) Ra5

Kluger vs. Sandor
Hungary 1954

Black to Play and Draw

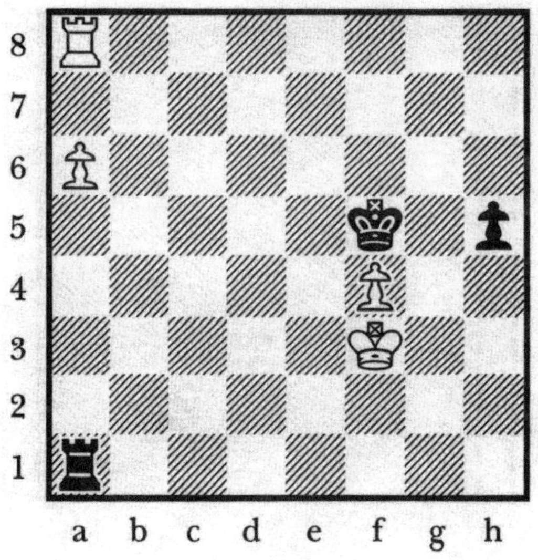

(a) Ra3+ (b) h4 (c) Kg6

Composed by Moravec

Black to Play and Draw

(a) Rh2 (b) Ra2 (c) Rb2

QUEEN ENDINGS

Queen vs. Rook

(a) Qh1+ (b) Qd8+ (c) Qh5+

Composed by Frink

White to Play and Draw

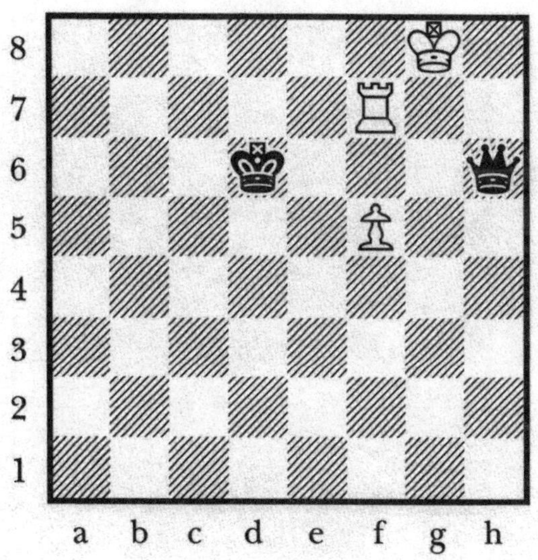

(a) Rf8 (b) Rh7 (c) Rg7

Composed by Troitsky

White to Play and Draw

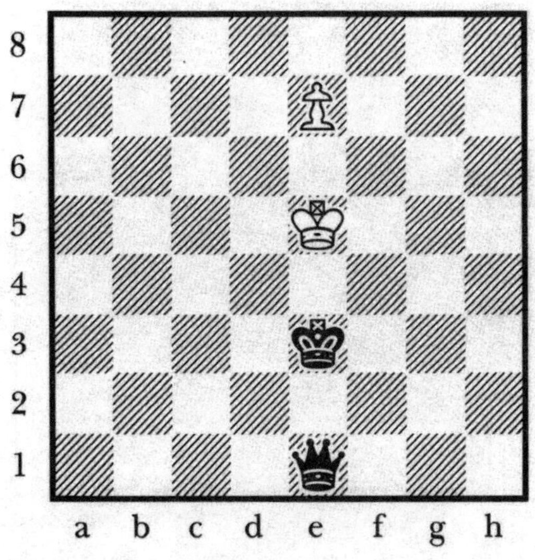

(a) Kd6 (b) Kf6 (c) Ke6

Composed by Lolli

White to Play and Win

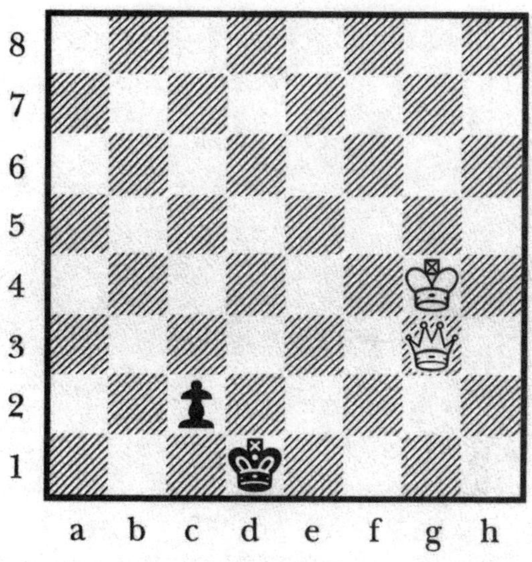

(a) Qd3+ (b) Qb3 (c) Qg1+

Composed by Horwitz

White to Play and Win

(a) Qd3 (b) Qh1+ (c) Qh6

Composed by Kling & Horowitz

White to Play and Win

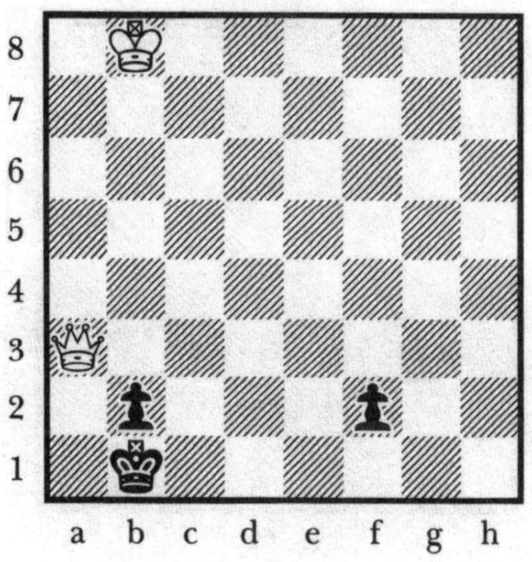

(a) Qa6 (b) Qf3 (c) Qd3+

Composed by Mandler

White to Play and Win

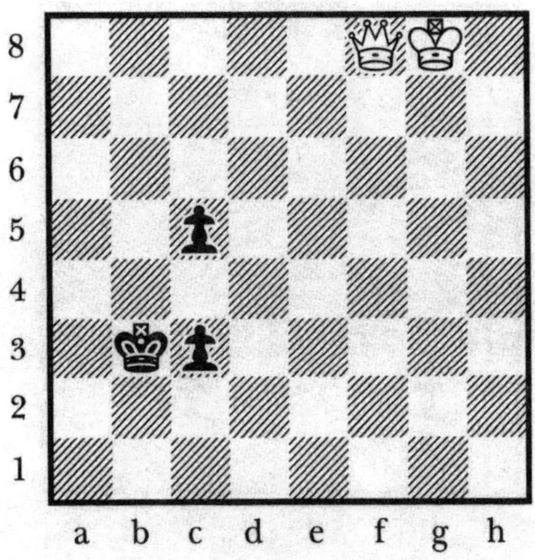

(a) Qxc5 (b) Qf4 (c) Qf3

Composed by Gorgiev

White to Play and Win

(a) Kb7 (b) Ka7 (c) Qe5+

Composed by Chekhover

White to Play and Draw

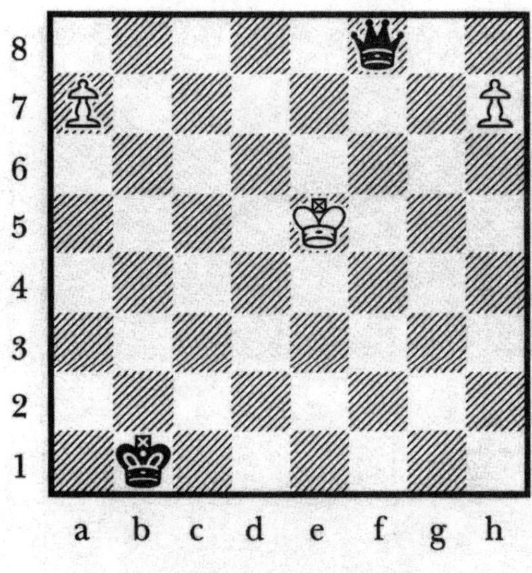

(a) Kd5 (b) Ke6 (c) a8/Q

Yates vs. Marshall
Carlsbad 1929

White to Play and Win

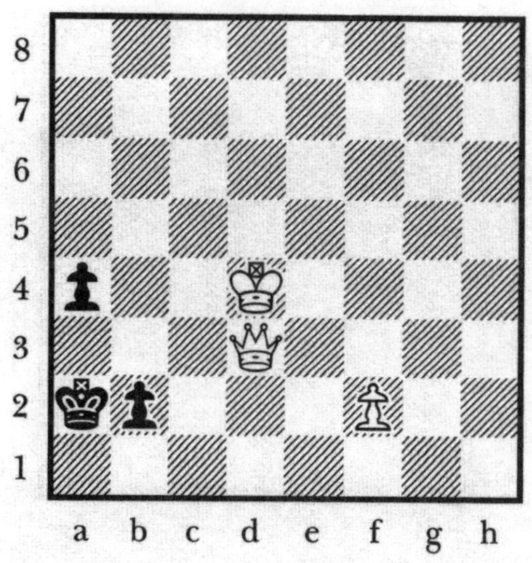

(a) Qc4+ (b) Kc4 (c) Qc2

Composed by Joseph

White to Play and Win

(a) Qg8 (b) Qe8 (c) Qf8

Composed by Berger

White to Play and Win

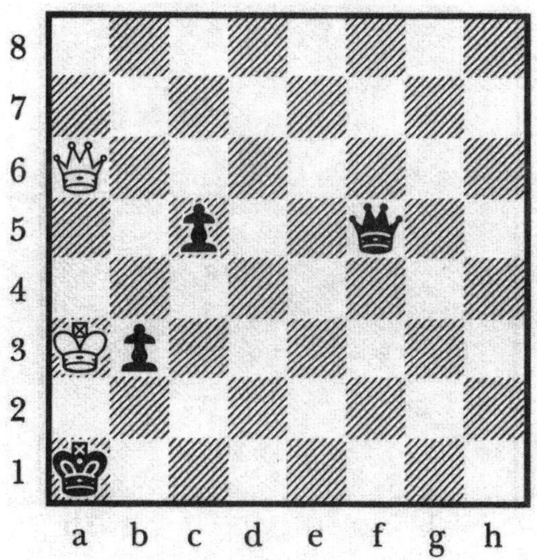

(a) Kxb3+ (b) Qc4 (c) Qe2

Composed by Kling & Horwitz

White to Play and Win

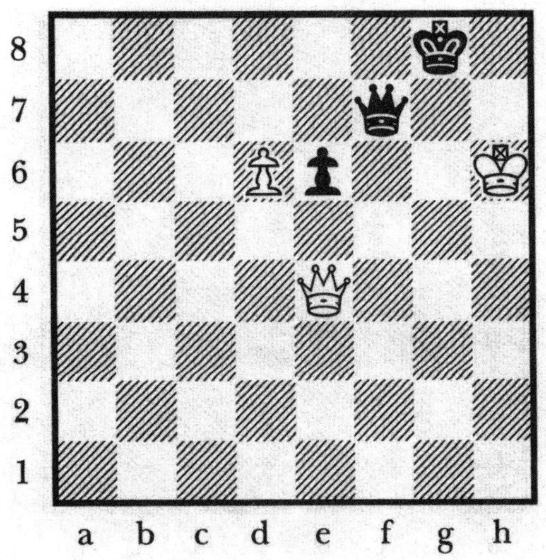

(a) Qg6+ (b) Qg2+ (c) Qa8+

Composed by Bekey

White to Play and Win

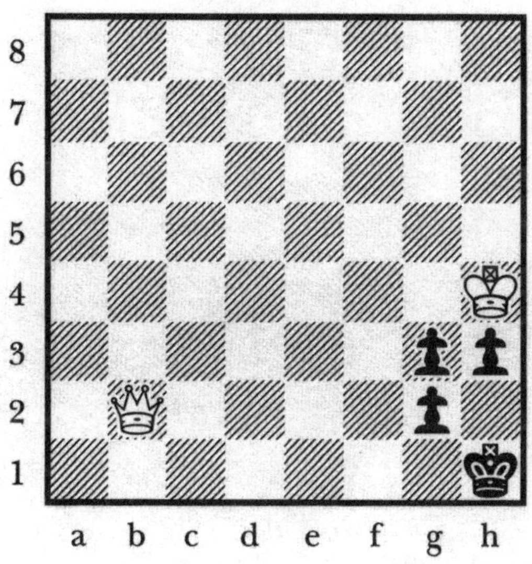

(a) Qb7 (b) Kxg3 (c) Kxh3

Composed by Rinck

White to Play and Win

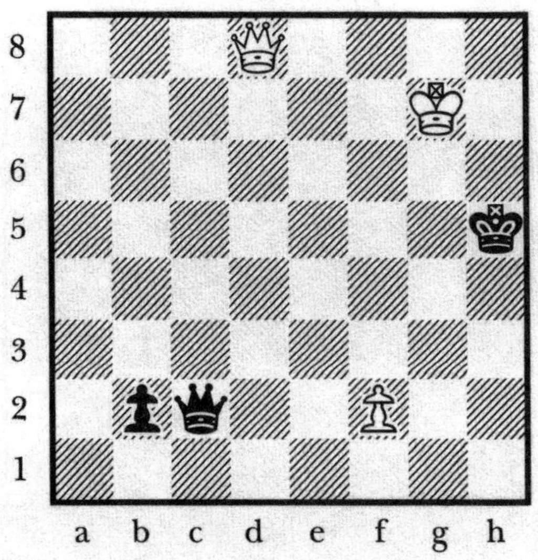

(a) Qh8+ (b) Qd5+ (c) Qe8+

Composed by Horwitz

White to Play and Win

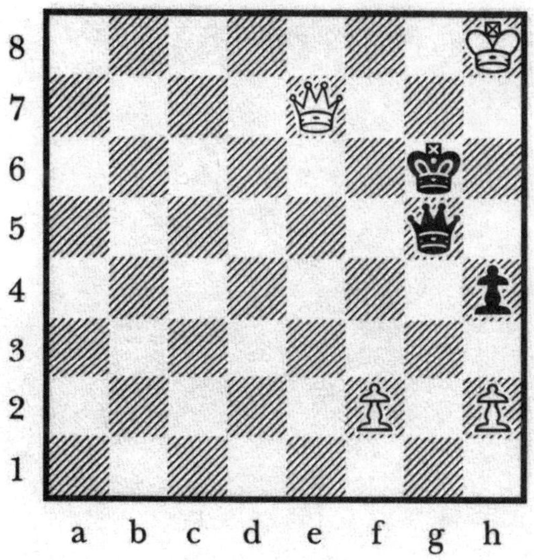

(a) Qxg5+ (b) Qg7+ (c) Qe6+

Composed by Rinck

White to Play and Win

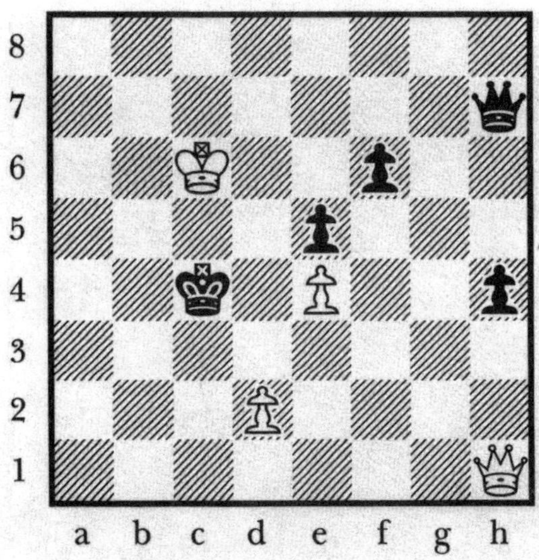

(a) Qb1 (b) Qf3 (c) Qc1+

Composed by Rinck

White to Play and Draw

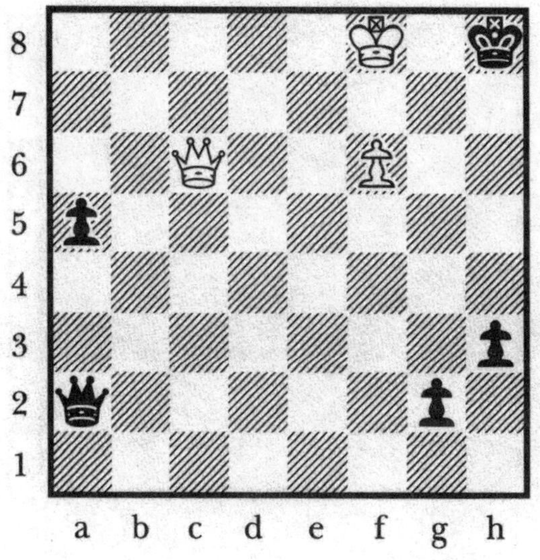

(a) Qe8 (b) Qc3 (c) f7

Becker vs. Moritz
Breslau 1925

White to Play and Win

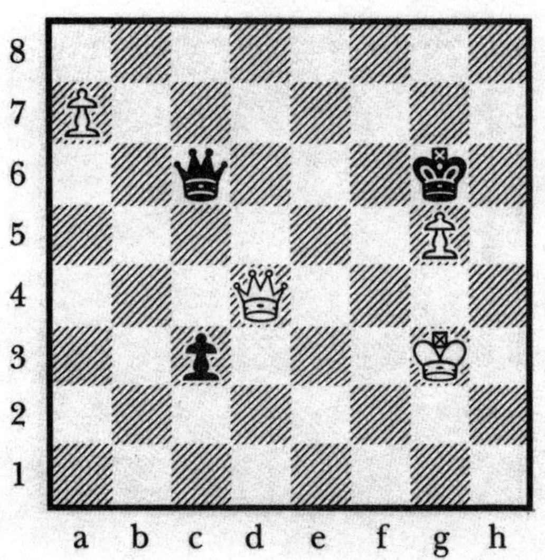

(a) Qh8 (b) a8/Q (c) Qf6+

Composed by Kubbel

White to Play and Win

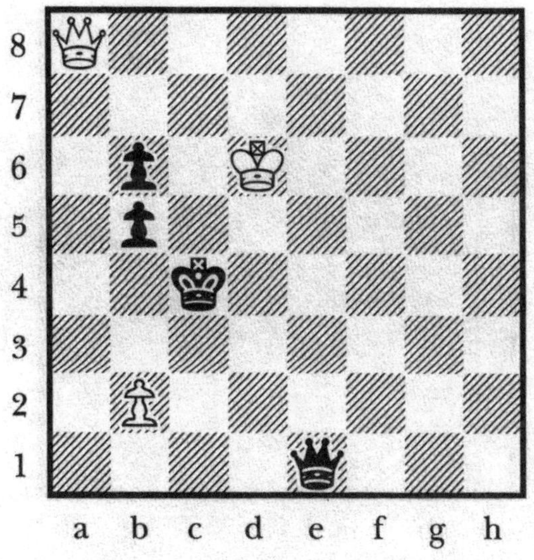

(a) Qa2+ (b) Qc6+ (c) Qd5+

Composed by Troitzky

White to Play and Win

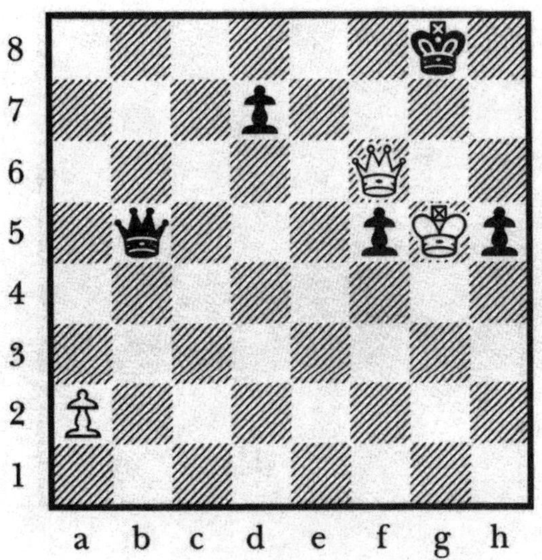

(a) Kh6 (b) Kg6 (c) Qxf5

Lichtenstein vs. Sternberg
Vienna 1923

White to Play and Win

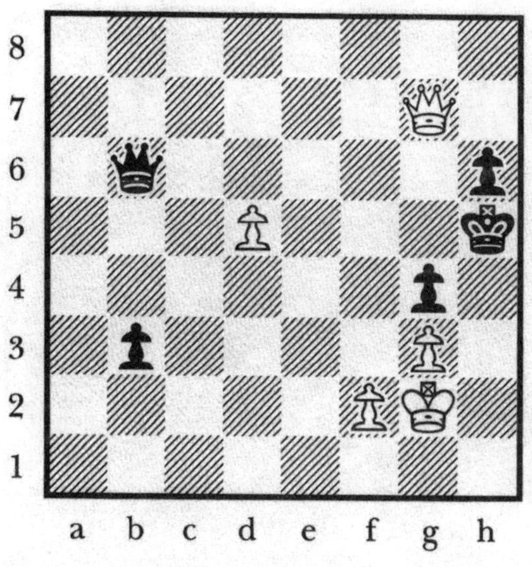

(a) Qe5+ (b) f3 (c) Qf7+

Composed by Cook

White to Play and Draw

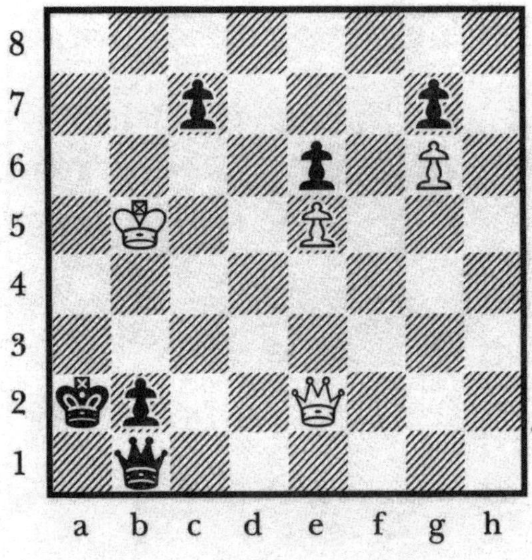

(a) Ka4 (b) Kb4 (c) Qc4+

Composed by Kling & Horwitz

White to Play and Win

(a) Qd5+ (b) Qb1+ (c) Qa6+

Composed by Kling & Horwitz

White to Play and Draw

(a) Qb8+ (b) Kg5 (c) Kg3

126

Composed by Kling & Horwitz

White to Play and Win

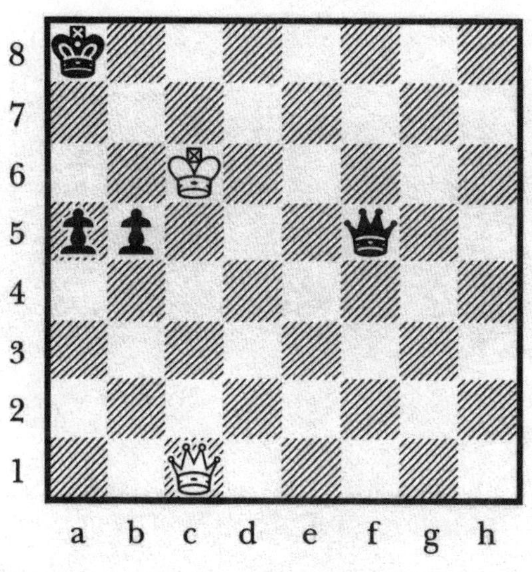

(a) Qh1 (b) Kb6 (c) Qh6

Stahlberg vs. Euwe
Stockholm 1937

White to Play and Draw

(a) Kg3 (b) h5 (c) Qb5

Composed by Horwitz

White to Play and Win

(a) Qe3+ (b) Qb4+ (c) Qb1+

Composed by Troitzky

White to Play and Win

(a) Qh8+ (b) Be4 (c) Bd5

Composed by Troitzky

White to Play and Win

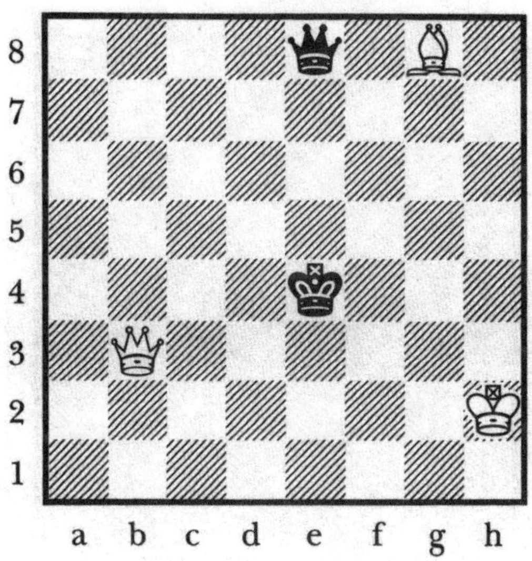

(a) Qd5+ (b) Bd5+ (c) Bh7+

Composed by Centurini

White to Play and Win

(a) Kh5 (b) Qf6+ (c) Qe5+

Composed by Troitzky

White to Play and Win

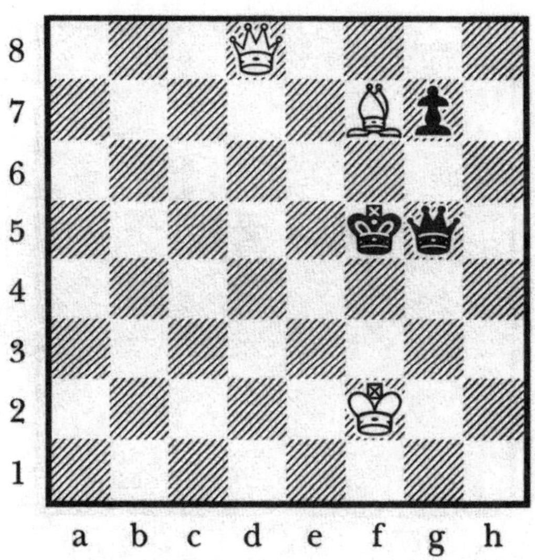

(a) Be6+ (b) Qd5+ (c) Qd3+

Composed by Horwitz

White to Play and Win

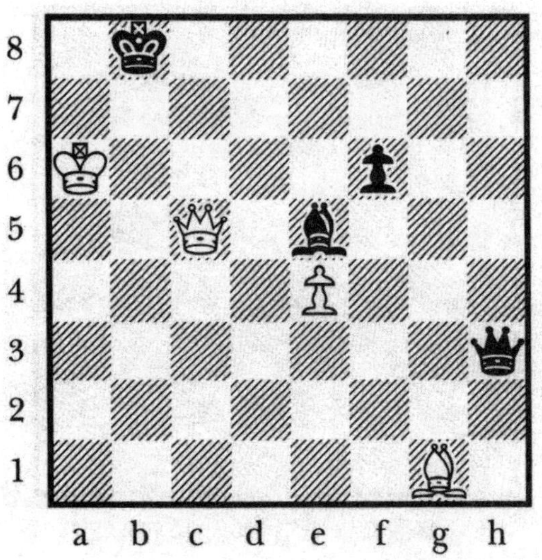

(a) Qb6+ (b) Qb5+ (c) Qf8+

Composed by Troitzky

White to Play and Win

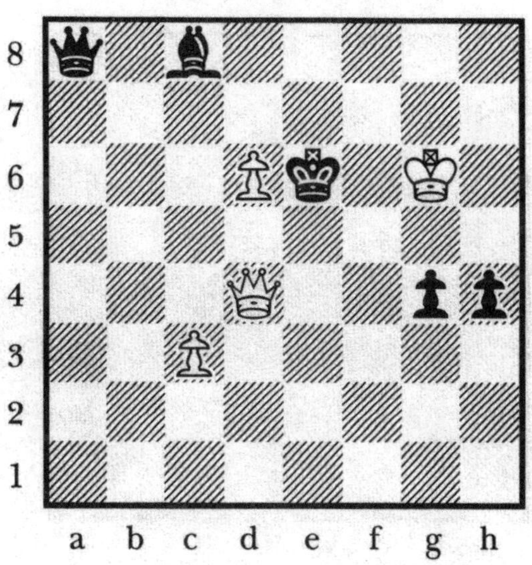

(a) Qf6+ (b) d7 (c) Qxg4+

Composed by Troitzky

White to Play and Win

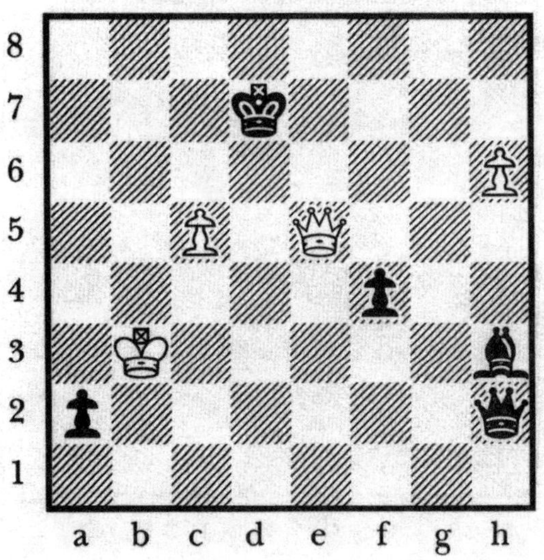

(a) c6+ (b) Qd6+ (c) h7

Composed by Prokes

White to Play and Win

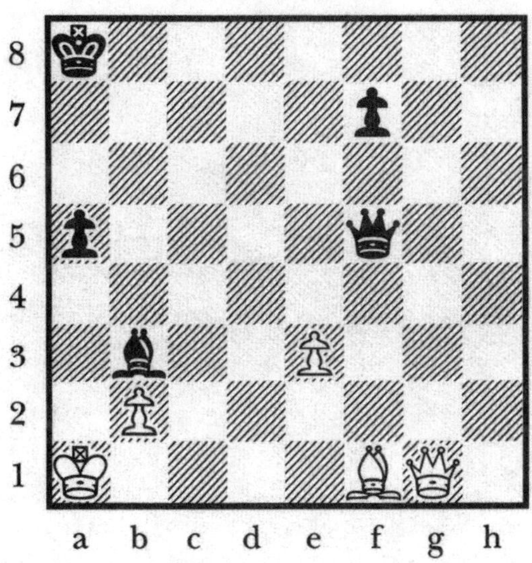

(a) e4 (b) Qg8+ (c) Bg2+

Composed by Troitzky

White to Play and Win

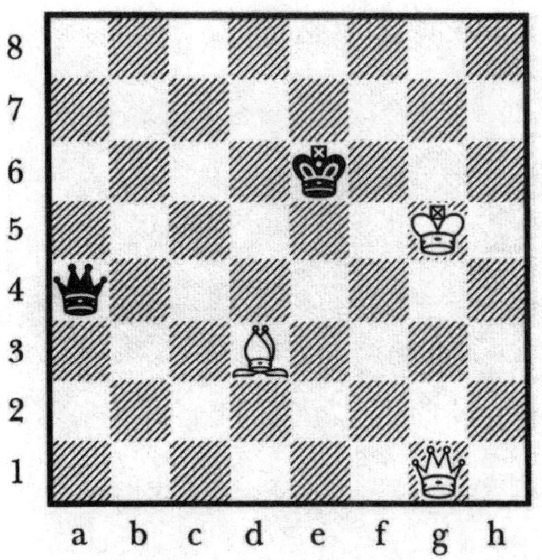

(a) Qc5 (b) Qb6+ (b) Bf5+

138

Composed by Kling & Horwitz

White to Play and Win

(a) Nxc1 (b) Ng3+ (c) Qe6+

Composed by Dehler

White to Play and Win

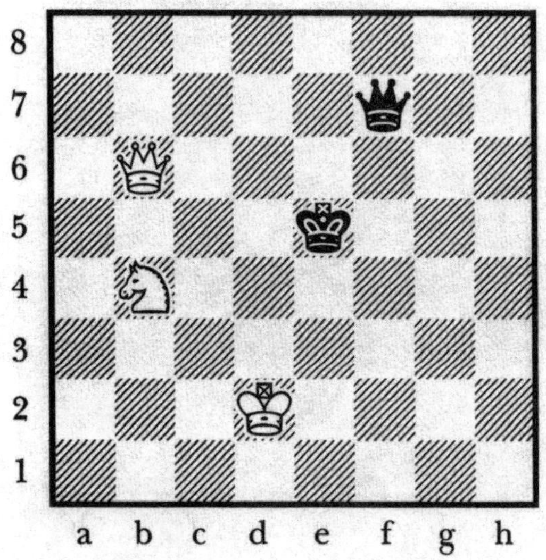

(a) Qe3+ (b) Nc6+ (c) Nd3+

Cited by Tattersall

White to Play and Win

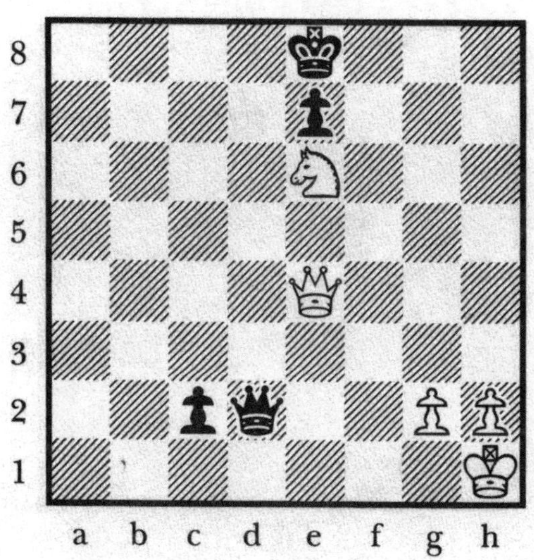

(a) Qg6+ (b) Qc6+ (c) Qa4+

Composed by Kubbel

White to Play and Win

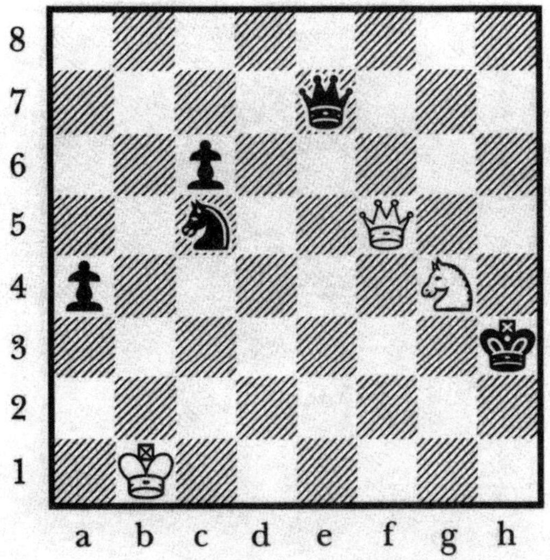

(a) Qf3+ (b) Ne5+ (c) Ne3+

Composed by Prokes

White to Play and Win

(a) Nc6+ (b) Nf5+ (c) Ne6+

Composed by Prokop

White to Play and Win

(a) Qf6 (b) Qg6+ (c) Qe6

Composed by Rinck

White to Play and Win

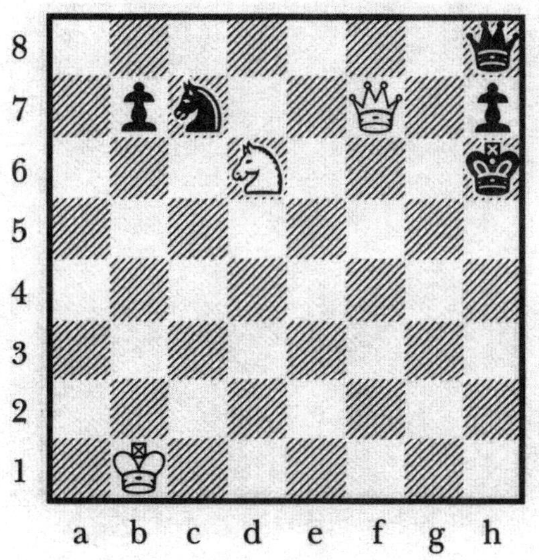

(a) Qxc7 (b) Qf3 (c) Qf4+

Composed by Lewitt

White to Play and Win

(a) Qh7+ (b) Qd3+ (c) Qb3+

Composed by Horwitz

White to Play and Win

(a) Kg8 (b) Kg7 (c) Kh6

Composed by Prokes

White to Play and Win

(a) Bf4+ (b) Be3 (c) Nc6+

Composed by Grigoriev

White to Play and Draw

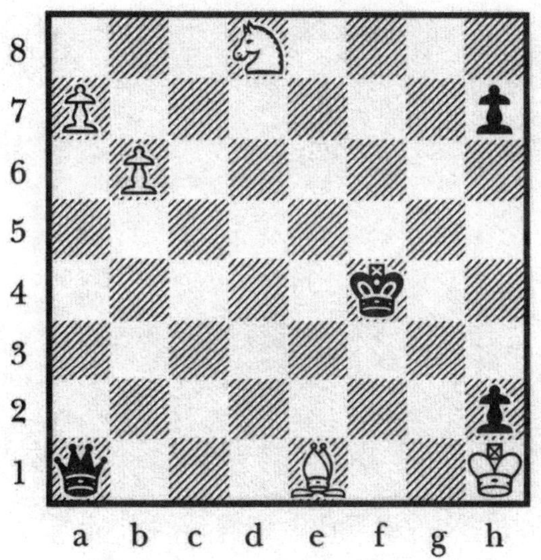

(a) b7 (b) a8/Q (c) Kxh2

Composed by Rinck

White to Play and Win

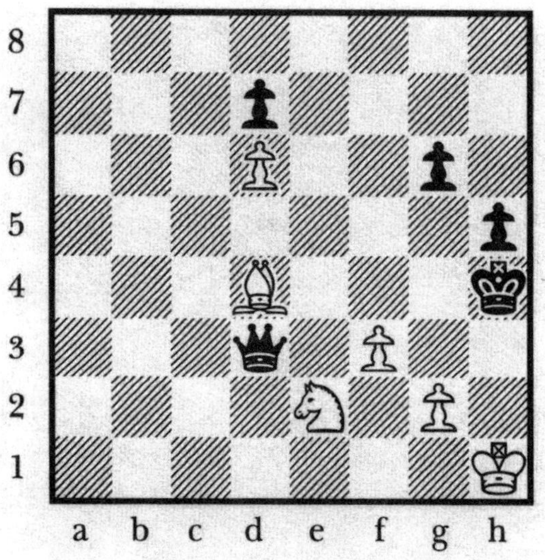

(a) g3+ (b) Bf2+ (c) Bf6+

Composed by Bowly

White to Play and Draw

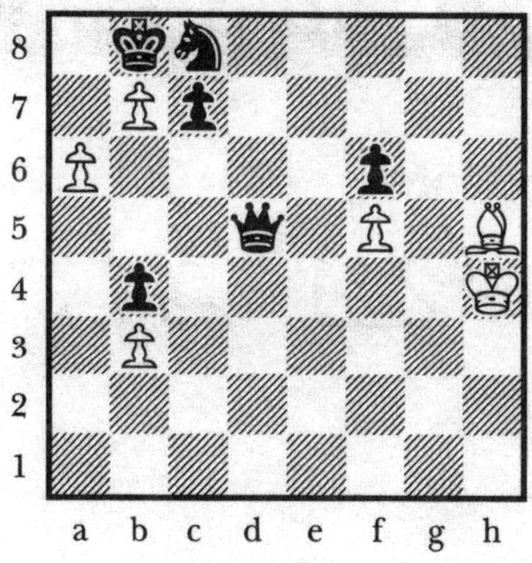

(a) a7+ (b) Bf3 (c) Kg3

MINOR PIECE ENDINGS

151

Dolmatov vs. Bologan
Calcutta 1999

White to Play and Draw

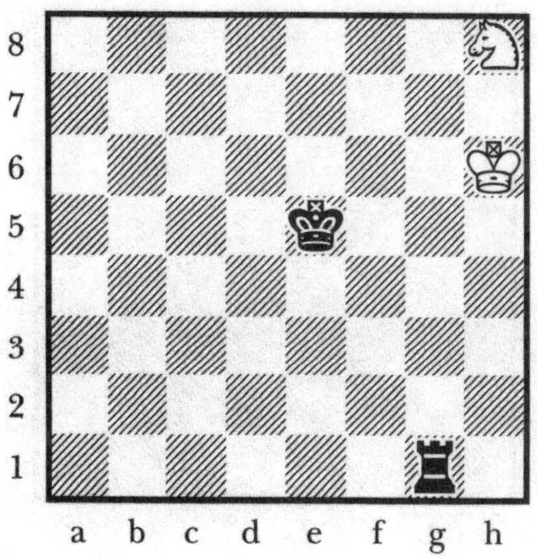

(a) Ng6+ (b) Nf7+ (c) Kh7

Composed by Benko

White to Play and Draw

(a) Bb8 (b) Bd6 (c) Kxe2

Composed by Frink

White to Play and Win

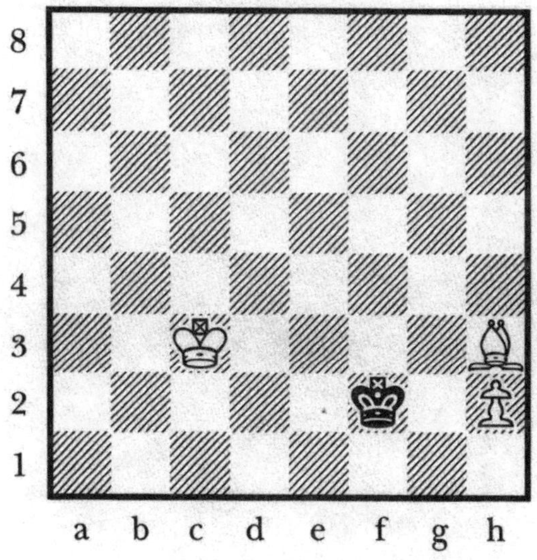

(a) Bd7 (b) Be6 (c) Bg2

Composed by Prokes

White to Play and Win

(a) h6 (b) Kb6 (c) Kb7

Composed by Quackenstadt

White to Play and Win

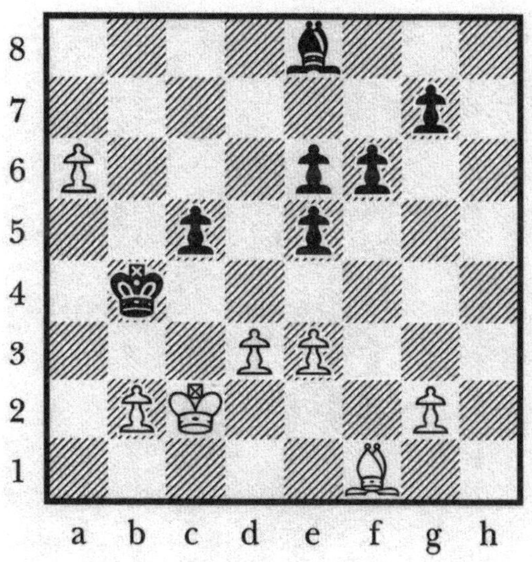

(a) a7 (b) Be2 (c) g4

Composed by Kubbel

White to Play and Draw

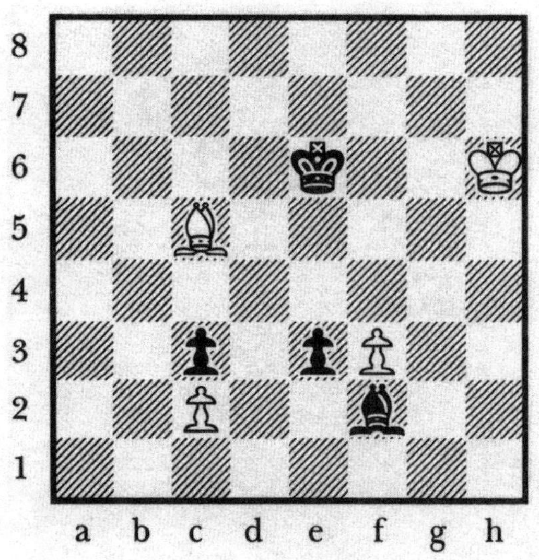

(a) Bd4 (b) Kg5 (c) Bb4

Composed by Prokes

White to Play and Win

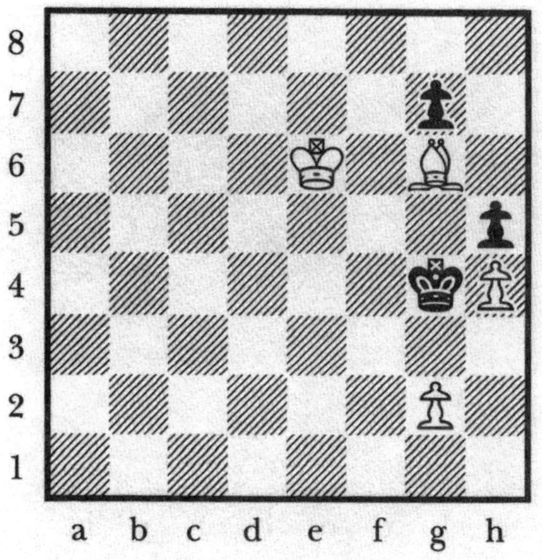

(a) Kf7 (b) Bf5+(c) Ke5

Composed by Prokes

White to Play and Win

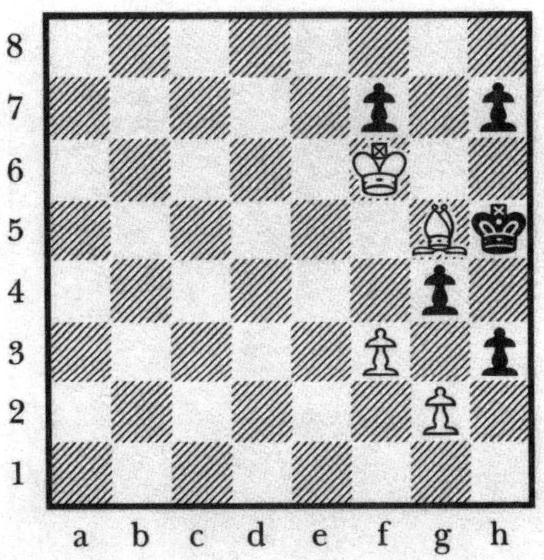

(a) Kf5 (b) fxg4+ (c) g3

Composed by Reti

White to Play and Draw

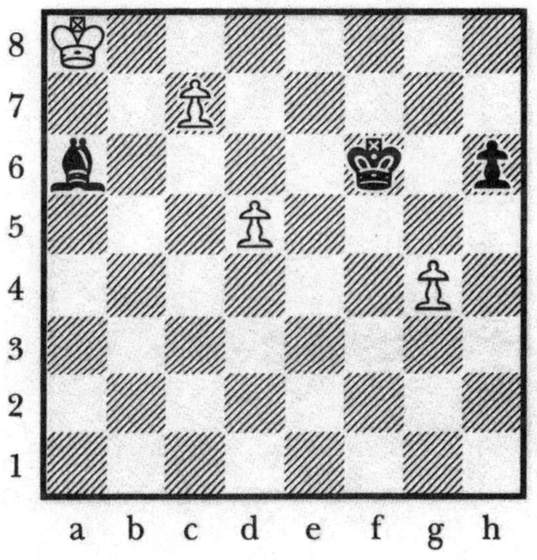

(a) d6 (b) Ka7 (c) Kb8

Composed by Branton

White to Play and Win

(a) Ke1 (b) Bb3 (c) Kf2

Composed by Peckover

White to Play and Win

(a) Bc1 (b) Bf6 (c) Be5

Composed by Mason

White to Play and Win

(a) g4+ (b) a7 (c) Ke3

Composed by Hoppe

White to Play and Win

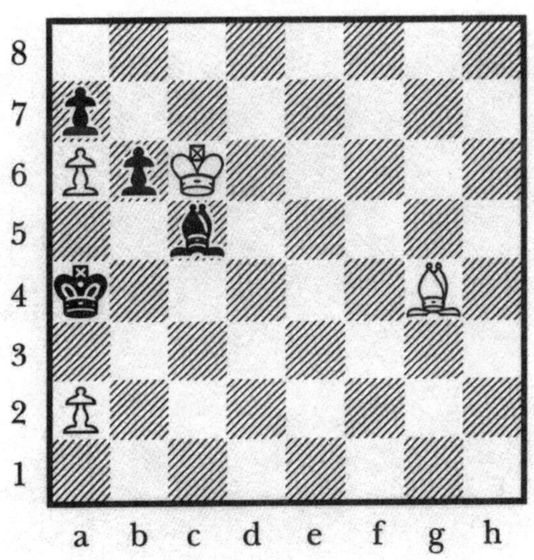

(a) Kb7 (b) Be6 (c) Be2

Composed by Kazantsev

White to Play and Win

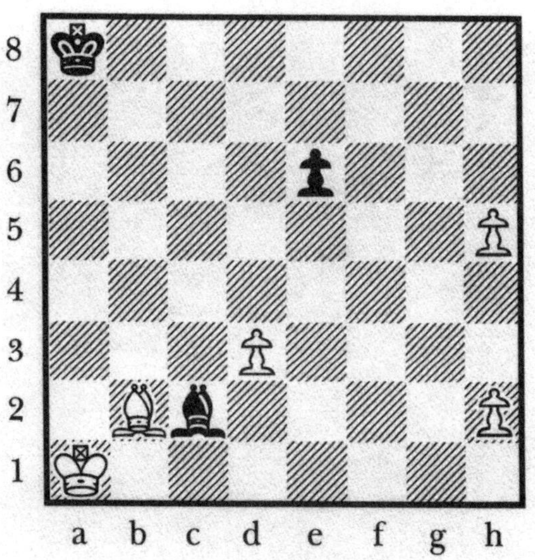

(a) Ba3 (b) Bh8 (c) h6

Composed by Herbstmann

White to Play and Win

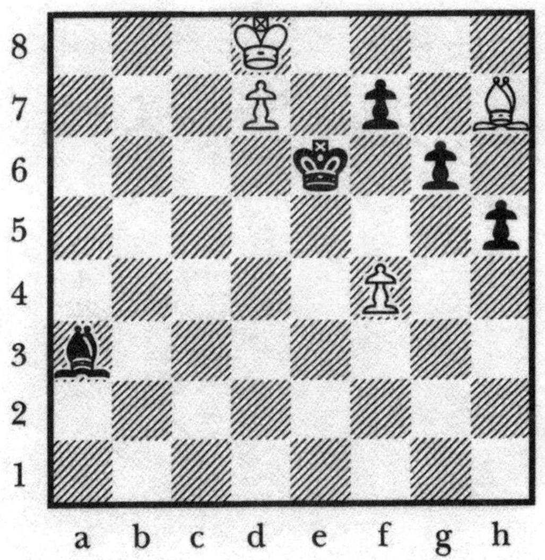

(a) Ke8 (b) Bg8 (c) f5+

Composed by Delimbourg

White to Play and Win

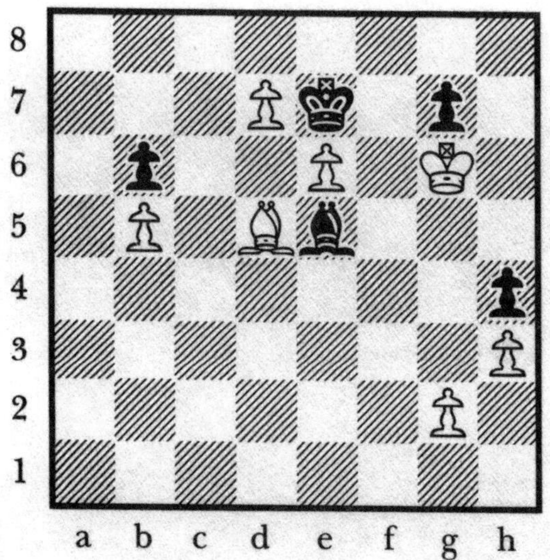

(a) Kf5 (b) d8/Q+ (c) g4

Composed by Norlin

White to Play and Win

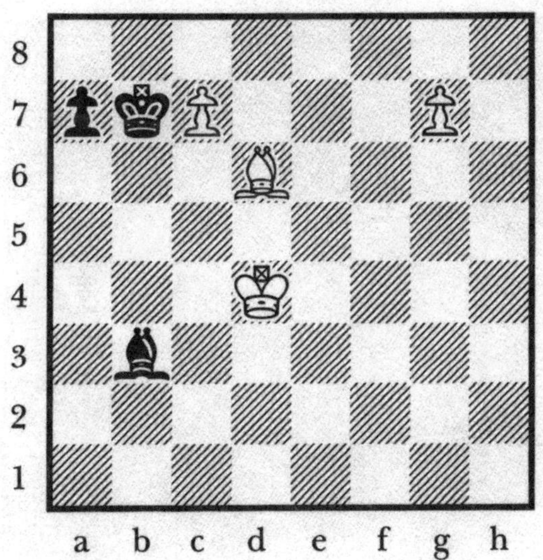

(a) Ke5 (b) Kc3 (c) Kc5

Walther vs. Fischer
Zurich 1959

White to Play and Win

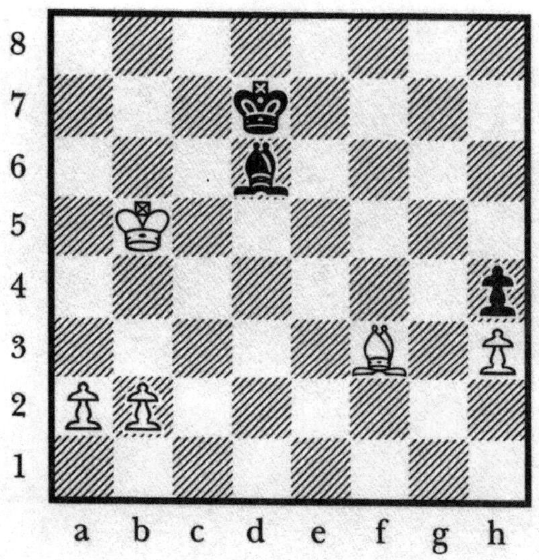

(a) a4 (b) b4 (c) a3

Composed by Reti

White to Play and Win

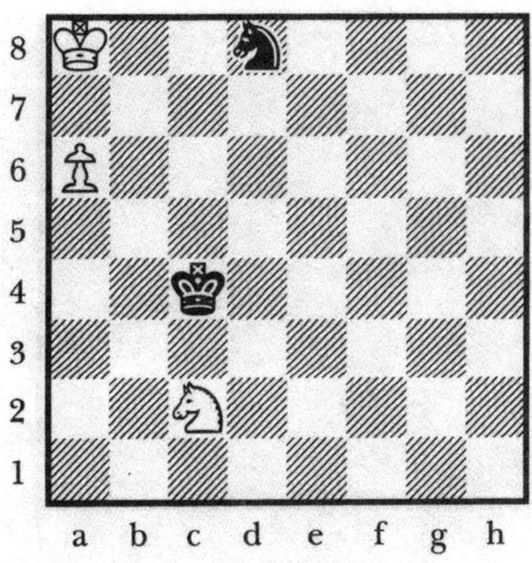

(a) a7 (b) Ka7 (c) Kb8

Composed by Rinck

White to Play and Draw

(a) Ne5 (b) Ne3+ (c) Nf2

Composed by Rinck

White to Play and Win

(a) Nc7+ (b) Nf6 (c) Nxd6

Composed by Platov

White to Play and Win

(a) a5 (b) Nc1 (c) Nxf4

Composed by Horwitz

White to Play and Win

(a) Ne3 (b) Kc1 (c) Nf2

Composed by Salvio

White to Play and Win

(a) Nxg7 (b) Nxh6 (c) Ne3

Composed by Troitzky

White to Play and Win

(a) Nd6 (b) d4 (c) Nxh6

Composed by Reichhelm

White to Play and Win

(a) Nf3 (b) Kb6 (c) Kc6

Composed by Larsen

White to Play and Win

(a) Kg7 (b) Nd4 (c) Nc3

Composed by Benko

White to Play and Draw

(a) a5 (b) Kb4 (c) Kc4

Composed by Branton

White to Play and Draw

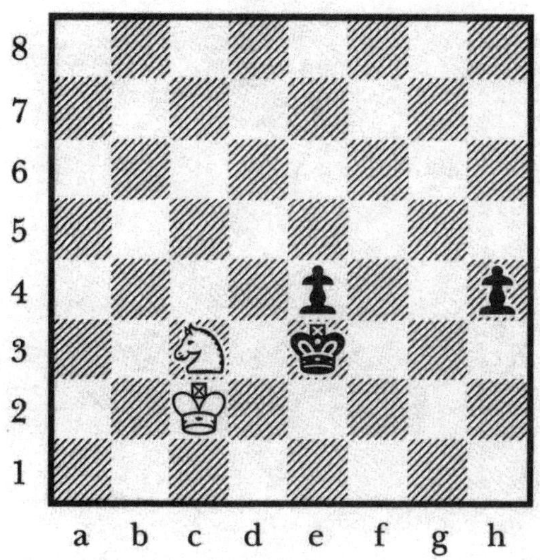

(a) Nd5+ (b) Nd1+ (c) Kd1

Composed by Halberstadt

White to Play and Win

(a) Kb4 (b) Kb2 (c) Kb3

Composed by Havasi

White to Play and Win

(a) h7 (b) Nc3+ (c) Kd5

Composed by Lommer

White to Play and Win

(a) Ne5 (b) Kxd8 (c) bxa4

Composed by Troitzky

White to Play and Win

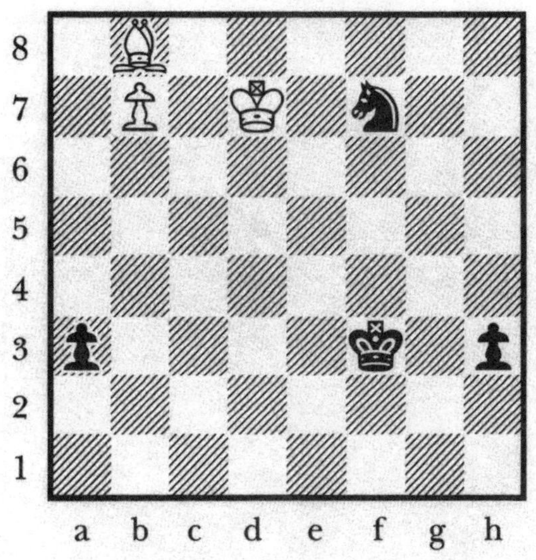

(a) Ba7 (b) Bg3 (c) Bh2

Fischer vs. Taimanov
Vancouver 1971

White to Play and Win

(a) Bf5+ (b) Bd1 (c) Bc8

Composed by Selesniev

White to Play and Win

(a) Kf7 (b) Kf5 (c) Kf6

Composed by Cook

White to Play and Win

(a) Nb6 (b) Ne5 (c) Nd6

Composed by Branton

White to Play and Win

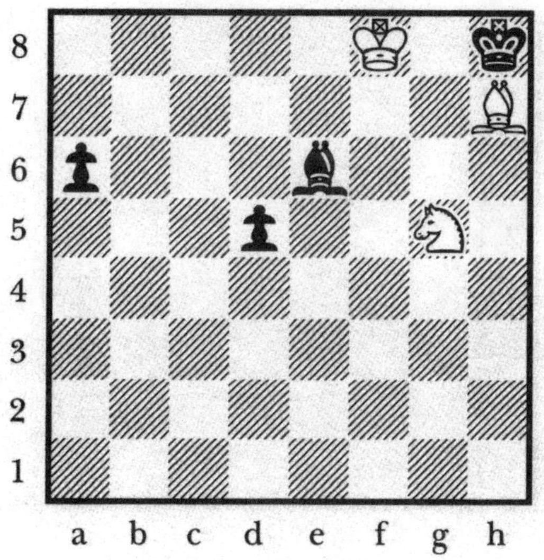

(a) Bb1 (b) Bc2 (c) Bd3

Composed by Loyd

White to Play and Draw

(a) Bd7 (b) Bc6+ (c) Ke2

Composed by Ulreich

White to Play and Win

(a) Kxd7 (b) Nh6 (c) g6

Composed by Loyd

White to Play and Win

(a) Kxg4 (b) Ne3 (c) Nh3

Composed by Bolton

White to Play and Win

(a) Nf2 (b) Nf3+ (c) Kf4

Composed by Hasse

White to Play and Draw

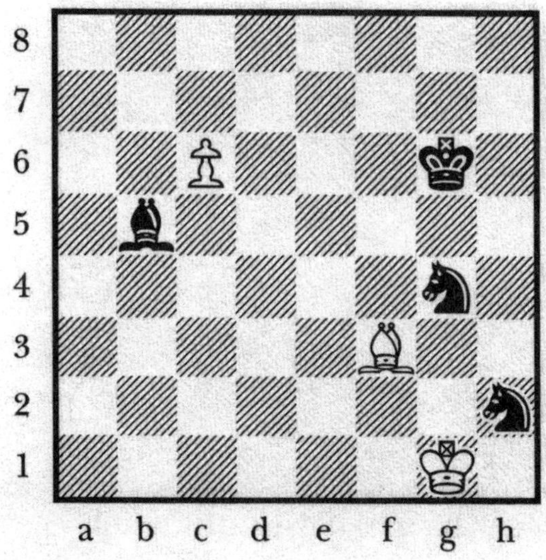

(a) Bxg4 (b) Be4+ (c) Kg2

193

Composed by Loyd

White to Play and Win

(a) Nxf2+ (b) Nfg3+ (c) Neg3+

Composed by Rombach

White to Play and Win

(a) Nb6 (b) Kh8 (c) N/4e5

Composed by Reichhelm

White to Play and Win

(a) Nc4 (b) Kc8 (c) Kc7

Composed by Benko

White to Play and Win

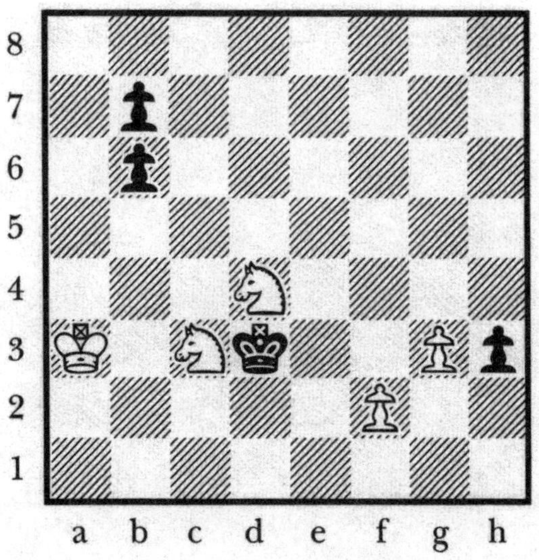

(a) f4 (b) Nf3 (c) Nd1

Composed by Platov

White to Play and Draw

(a) Bd8 (b) Nc3 (c) Nd2

Composed by Rinck

White to Play and Win

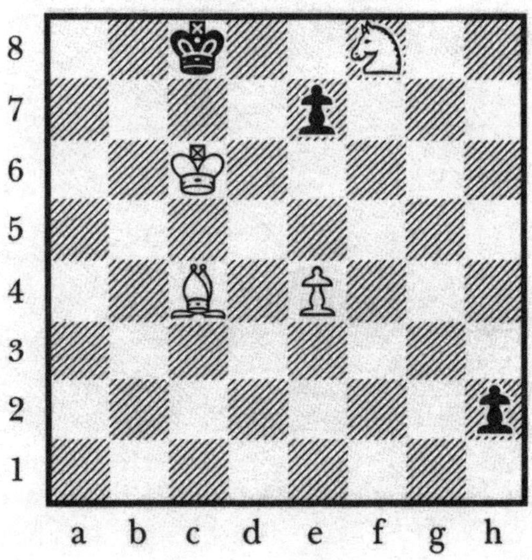

(a) Be6+ (b) Ba6+ (c) Ne6

Composed by Rinck

White to Play and Win

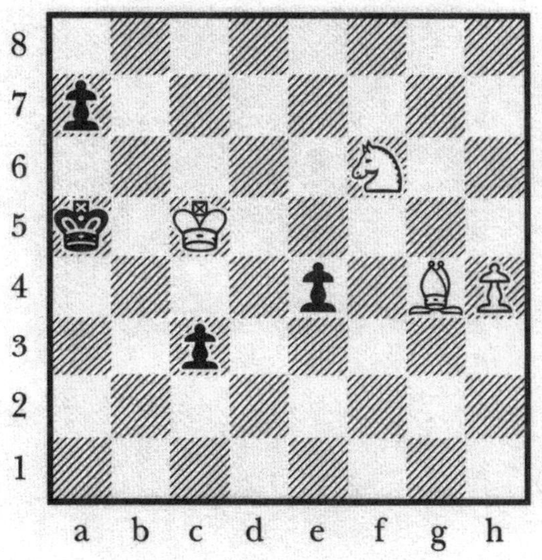

(a) Nxe4 (b) Bd1 (c) Nd5

Composed by Rinck

White to Play and Win

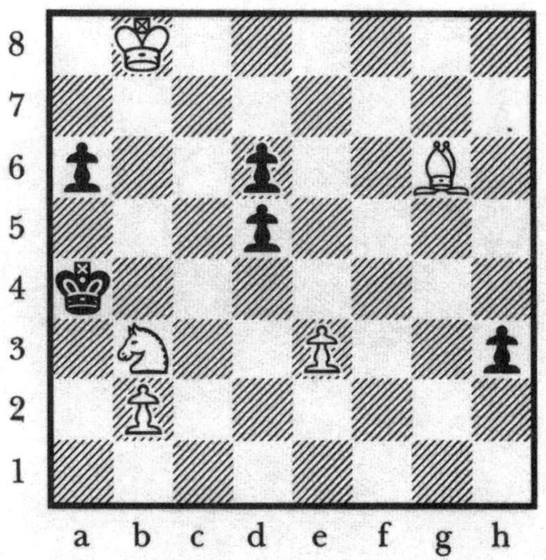

(a) Nc1 (b) Bf7 (c) Nd4

THE SOLUTIONS

1. A is the correct answer.
Choices: (a) Ke3 (b) Ke4 (c) Kf4

(a) This basic position illustrates the vital importance of the "opposition" and why stalemate is such a valuable resource for the defender. When opposing kings stand on the same file, rank or diagonal, and are an odd number of squares apart, whoever is NOT on move "has the opposition." Whoever must move is said to "lose the opposition."

If Black can keep his king in front of his pawn before pushing it too far, he wins. If not, he draws. It's as simple at that.

All moves lose the opposition except 1 Ke3! (putting it an odd number of squares away from Black's king on the same file) Ke6 (or 1...Kf6 2 Kf4) 2 Ke4 Kf6 3 Kf4 Kg6 4 Kg4 f5+ 5 Kf4 Kf6 6 Kf3 Kg5 7 Kg3 f4+ 8 Kf3 Kf5 9 Ke2 Kg4 10 Kf2 f3 11 Kf1! (but not 11 Kg1? Kg3 gaining the opposition 12 Kf1 f2 13 Ke2 Kg2 and wins) Kg3 12 Kg1 (keeping the opposition until the very last breath) f2+ 13 Kf1 Kf3 stalemate — the saving resource!

(b) After 1 Ke4? Ke6 2 Kf4 Kf6 White has lost the opposition and must give ground. No matter where he goes, Black can get his king in front of the pawn and usher it to the queening square (see "c").

(c) A dilemma occurs after 1 Kf4? Kf6 2 Kf3 (or 2 Ke4 Kg5 3 Kf3 Kf5) Kf5 3 Ke3 Kg4 4 Kf2 Kf4 5 Ke2 Kg3 6 Kf1 Kf3 7 Ke1 Kg2 8 Ke2 f5 and the queening path is clear now that White can no longer erect a blockade.

2. C is the correct answer.
Choices: (a) Kf4 (b) Kf5 (c) g5

(a) Black is a pawn down but achieves his goal on 1 Kf4? g5+ 2 Kf3= (stalemate).

(b) No king move wins. Again on 1 Kf5? g5 there is no way to pry Black loose from his self-imposed casket.

(c) In chess, as in advertising, it often pays to give a little to get a lot.. Sacrificing a pawn snuffs out stalemate once and for all: 1 g5! Kxg5 2 Ke4 Kh5 3 Kf3! (not 4 Kf4? Kh4 5 Kf3 g5=) Kh4 4 Kf4 g6 5 Ke3 Kg5 6 Kf3 Kh4 7 Kf4 g5+ 8 Kf3 Kh5 9 Kxg3 and wins.

3. A is the correct answer.
Choices: (a) Ka3 (b) Kc3 (c) Kc2

(a) White's first task is to reach the diagram with Black on move. To do so White must lose a move. This involves a maneuver known as triangulation. Step one is 1 Ka3! Kb6 2 Kb2! Ka5 3 Kb3! Bingo! White's king danced in a small triangle (a3-b2-b3) and now Black is on move instead of White. 3...Kb6 4 Kc3 Ka5 5 Kd2! (the winning touch; careless is 5 Kd3? Kb4!) 5...Ka5 6 Ke3! Kb4 7 Kd3 Ka3 8 Ke4 Kxa2 9 Kd5 Kb3 10 Kxc5.

(b) The direct approach to c5 fails 1 Kc3? Ka4! 2 Kd3 Kb4! and White can make no progress (3 a3+ Kxa3 4 Ke4 Kb3! 5 Kd5? Kb4 actually wins for Black).

(c) Fruitless is 1 Kc2? Ka4! 2 Kd2 (or 2 Kd3 Kb4!) Ka3 3 Kd3 (or 3 Ke3 Kxa2) Kb4!=.

4. A is the correct answer.
Choices: (a) Kg1 (b) Kg3 (c) a6

(a) Retreating is the only way to win: 1 Kg1! Kd4 2 a6 Ke3 3 Kf1! blockades the Black pawn while queening the White pawn.

(b) 1 Kg3? looks natural but permits a neat draw by 1...Kd4! 2 a6 (if 2 Kxf3 Kc5 gets back in time to gobble the pawn) Ke3 3 a7 f2 4 a8/Q f1/Q=.

(c) The hasty 1 a6? throws away the win after 1...Kd2! 2 a7 f2 3 Kg2 Ke2 4 a8/Q f1/Q+ with material equality.

5. B is the correct answer.
Choices: (a) Kd7 (b) Kd5 (c) Kd6

(a) Taking the bull by the horns by going straight for the pawn allows a draw after 1 Kd7? Kd4 2 Kc6 Ke5 3 Kb7 Kd6 4 Kxa7 Kc7 5 Ka8 Kc8 6 a7 stalemate.

(b) The diagonal route 1 Kd5! restricts access to the key d4 square. On 1...Kb4 2 Kc6 Ka5 3 Kb7 Kb5 4 Kxa7 Kc6 5 Kb8 Kb6 6 a7 and the pawn queens.

(c) The actual game was only drawn after 1 Kd6? Kd4 2 Kc6 Ke5! 3 Kb7 Kd6 4 Kxa7 Kc7 (as in "a") and White's king is entombed.

6. B is the correct answer.
Choices: (a) b4 (b) Kb1 (c) Ka2

(a) Too hasty is 1 b4? Kg2 2 Kb2 Kf3 3 Kc3 Ke4 4 Kc4 (no better is 4 b5 b6) Ke5 5 Kc5 Ke6 6 Kb6 (if 6 b5 Kd7 7 Kb6 Kc8 holds) Kd5 7 Kxb7 Kc4= picking up the last button.

(b) White must improve the position of his king before touching his pawn. The winning idea is 1 Kb1! Kg2 2 Kc2 Kf3 3 Kd3! Kf4 4 Kd4 Kf5 5 Kd5 Kf6 6 Kd6 Kf7 7 b4 Ke8 8 Kc7 b5 9 Kc6 Kd810 Kxb5 Kc7 11 Ka6 Kb8 12 b5 Ka8 (if 12...Kc7 13 Ka7 ushers the pawn in) 13 b6 Kb8 14 b7 Kc7 15 Ka7 and queens.

(c) Inadequate is 1 Ka2? Kg2 2 Kb3 Kf3 3 Kc4 Ke4! 4 Kc5 Ke5 5 b4 Ke6 6 Kb5 Kd5 7 Kxb7 Kc4 as in "a".

7. C is the correct answer.
Choices: (a) Kd3 (b) Kc3 (c) Kb1

(a) No threat is posed by 1 Kd3? Ke5 2 Kc4 a3! 3 bxa3 Kd6 4 Kb5 Kc7=.

(b) Curiously, natural-looking moves often toss away the

advantage. If 1 Kc3? a3! 2 bxa3 (also drawn is 2 b4 Ke5 3 Kb3 Kd5 4 Kxa3 Kc6 5 Ka4 Kb6 and White can't get his king in front of his pawn) Ke6=.

(c) White must capture the pawn in such a way as to keep his king in front of his own pawn. Correct is 1 Kb1! a3! 2 b3! (wrongo is 2 b4? Ke5 3 Ka2 Kd5 4 Kxa3 Kc6 5 Ka4 Kb6=) Ke5 3 Ka2 Kd5 4 Kxa3 Kc6 5 Ka4! Kb6 6 Kb4 keeping the opposition and wins.

8. A is the correct answer.
Choices: (a) Kd4 (b) Kd5 (c) Ke5

(a) The paradoxical 1 Kd4! wins the pawn by not approaching it too soon while controlling the key c4 square. If 1...Kc6 2 Ke5 Kc5 3 f4! Kc4 4 Kf6 wins.

(b) Inadequate is 1 Kd5? Kb4 2 Kd4 Kb3! 3 f4 Kc2 4 Ke5 Kd3 5 Kf6 Ke4=.

(c) The straightforward 1 Ke5? Kc4 2 Kf6 Kd3 3 Kxg6 Ke4 4 Kg5 Kf3 picks up the last pawn to draw.

9. C is the correct answer.
Choices: (a) Kb8 (b) Kb7 (c) Kb6

(a) It rarely makes sense to decentralize the king, and this is no exception. Black draws after 1 Kb8? Kc3! 2 Kc7 Kd4 3 Kd7 Ke5 4 Kxe7 Kxf5.

(b) The same dilemma arises on 1. Kb7? Kc3! 2 Kc6 Kd4 3 Kd7 Ke5=.

(c) The vital difference reveals itself after 1 Kb6! Kc3! 2 Kc5! Kd2 (Black no longer has access to d4) 3 Kc6! (too hasty is 3 Kd5? Ke3 4 Ke6 Kf4! 5 e3+ Ke4 6 Kxe7 Kxf5=) Ke3 4 Kd5! (not 4 Kd7? Ke4! 5 Ke6 Kf4 6 e3+ Ke4=) Kf4 5 Ke6 Ke4 6 e3! Kxe3 (zugzwang) 7 Kxe7 Ke4 8 Kxf6 and the pawn queens.

10. B is the correct answer.
Choices: (a) Kd5 (b) Kf5 (c) Kf6

(a) This is a good example of how moves can be eliminated simply by making a mathematical count. Too slow is 1 Kd5? f5 2 Kc6 f4 3 Kxb6 f3 4 Kc7 f2 5 b6 f1/Q 6 b7 Qc4+ 7 Kd8 Qb5 8 Kc7 Qc5+ 9 Kd8 Qd6+ 10 Kc8 Qc6+ 11 Kb8 Kg5 and Black keeps repeating the process until his king closes in for the kill.

(b) Both sides must play sharply. Correct is 1 Kf5! Kh4 2 Kf4 Kh3 3 Kf3 Kh2 4 Kf2 f6 5 Kf3 Kg1 6 Ke4! Kf2! (not 6...Kg2? 7 Kf5 wins for White) 7 Kd5! f5 8 Kc6 and both sides queen, leading to a draw.

(c) Going directly for the pawn loses after 1 Kf6? Kg4 2 Kxf7 Kf5 3 Ke7 Ke5 8 Kd7 Kd5 5 Kc7 Kc5.

11. C is the correct answer.
Choices: (a) g6 (b) h6 (c) f6

(a) White actually loses after 1 g6? h6 2 Kd3 Kxf5.

(b) White only draws after 1 h6? gxh6 2 g6 hxg6 3 fxg6 Kf6 4 Kd3.

(c) The only way to create a passed pawn that can't be stopped is 1 f6! gxf6 2 g6! hxg6 3 h6!

12. A is the correct answer.
Choices: (a) Kg4 (b) g6 (b) h5

(a) Never give up the ship! In the game White did —a rare case of premature resignation. He overlooked a miracle draw by 1 Kg4! Ke5 2 g6! h6 (if 2...hxg6 3 fxg6 f5+ 4 Kg5 f4 5 h5 f3 6 h6 gxh6+ 7 Kxh6 f2 8 g7 and both sides queen) 3 Kh5 Kxf5 stalemate!

(b) Hopeless is 1 g6? h5! 2 Kf3 Ke5 and Black grazes on

pawns for dessert.

(c) Equally futile is 1 h5? h6 2 gxh6 gxh6 3 Kf3 Ke5 4 Kg4 Ke4 5 Kg3 Kxf5 mopping up.

13. B is the correct answer.
Choices: (a) Kg2 (b) c5 (c) f3

(a) White lost by 1 Kg2? Kf5 2 c5 g5! 3 Kh3 Ke5 4 c6 (no better is 4 f4+ gxf4 5 Kxh4 Kd5 6 Kg4 Kxc5 7 Kxf4 Kd4 8 Kf3 Kc3) Kd6 5 c7 Kxc7 6 f4 gxf4 7 Kxh4 Kd6 8 Kg4 Ke5.

(b) The drawing resource is 1 c5! Kf5 2 f4! (to stop g5 once and for all) Ke6 3 Kg2 Kd5 4 Kh3 Kxc5 5 Kxh4 Kd4 6 Kg5 Kc3 7 Kg6 Kb2 8 Kxg7 Kxa2 9 f5 b3=.

(c) The pointless 1 f3? loses a vital tempo (by contrast 1 f4! Kf5 2 c5! would transpose into "b") Kf5 2 Kg2 g5 with lines similar to "a."

14. A is the correct answer.
Choices:(a) Ka6 (b) Kc5 (c) b3

(a) It's necessary to force Black to push his d-pawn by triangulation: 1 Ka6! d6! (the best defense; if 1...d5 2 Kb5 Kb7 3 Kc5 d4 4 Kxd4 Kxb6 5 Kc4 Kc6 6 Kb4 Kb6 7 b3 gains the opposition) 2 Ka5! (the only way; not 2 b7? d5 3 Kb5 Kxb7 4 Kc5 Ka6! holds; or 2 Kb5? Kb7 3 Ka5 d5 4 Kb5 d4=) Ka8 3 Kb4 Kb8 4 Ka4 Ka8 5 Ka5 Kb8 6 Ka6 d5 7 Kb5 wins.

(b) The tempting 1 Kc5? Kb7 2 b3 Ka6 3 b4 Kb7 4 Kb5 d5 5 Kc5 d4 6 Kxd4 Kxb6 7 Kc4 Kc6 draws because White pushed his last pawn too soon.

(c) Wrong is 1 b3? Kb7 2 Kc5 d6+ 3 Kb5 d5 4 Kc5 d4 5 Kxd4 Kxb6 6 Kc4 Kc6 7 Kb4 Kb6 and Black holds the opposition because White no longer can gain a tempo by b3.

15. C is the correct answer.
Choices: (a) b6 (b) Kb4 (c) Ka6

(a) 1 b6? Kb7! 2 bxc7 Kxc7 leads to nought.

(b) Insufficient is 1 Kb4? Kb7 2 Kc5 f4 3 Kd4 Kb6 4 Ke4 Kxb5 5 Kxf4 c5 6 g4 Kc6 7 g5 Kd6=.

(c) Correct is 1 Ka6! Kb8 (if 1...f4 2 b6! c6 3 b7+ Kb8 4 Kb6 c5 5 Kxc5 Kxb7 6 Kd5 wins) 2 g3! Ka8 (no better is 2...Kc8 3 Ka7 Kd8 4 Kb8! Kd7 5 Kb7 Kd8 6 Kc6 Kc8 7 Kd5 Kb7 8 Ke5 Kb6 9 Kxf4 Kxb5 10 g4 c5 11 g5 c4 12 Ke4!) 3 b6 Kb8 4 Kb5! Kb7 5 bxc7 Kxc7 6 Kc5 Kd8 7 Kd6! wins (but not 7 Kd4? f4!).

16. A is the correct answer.
Choices: (a) Kf3 (b) Kf5 (c) Kd4

(a) Despite a material deficit, White can force an amazing win by 1 Kf3! b5 2 e4 b4 3 Ke2! b3 4 Kd1! Kg3 5 e5 dxe5 6 d6 e4 7 d7 e3 (if White had moved his king to d2 on move 4, this push would be accompanied by check with a draw after 8 Kxe3 b2) 8 d8/Q and wins.

(b) Not 1 Kf5? b5 2 e4 b4 3 e5 b3 4 exd6 b2 5 d7 b1/Q queening with check!

(c) White perishes after 1 Kd4? Kg3 2 e4 Kf4.

17. A is the correct answer.
Choices: (a) Kg2 (b) Ke2 (b) h5

(a) White is in peril because his king is so passive, yet he can draw by 1 Kg2! Kc4 (useless is 1...h5 2 Kf2! keeping the opposition) 2 h5! gxh5 3 Kh3 Kd4 4 Kh4 Ke4 5 Kxh5 Kf3 6 Kg5 Kxg3 7 Kxf5.

(b) Trying to keep Black's king from penetrating is futile: 1 Ke2? Kc4 2 Ke3 Kc3 3 Ke2 Kc2 4 Ke3 Kd1 5 Kf3 h5! 6 Kf2 Kd2 7 Kg2 Ke2 8 Kh3 Kf3 9 Kh2 Kf2 10 Kh3 Kg1 and White — in zugzwang — must commit hari kari by 11 g4.

(c) Insufficient is 1 h5? gxh5 2 Kg2 h4! 3 gxh4 Kc3 and Black's king will prevail on the kingside.

18. C is the correct answer.
Choices: (a) Kf6 (b) Kf7 (c) Ke7

(a) This is sticky because Black is aiming for stalemate after 1 Kf6? f4! 2 exf4 g5 3 fxg5=.

(b) The same goes for 1 Kf7? f4!

(c) This defense no longer works against 1 Ke7! Kh6 (offers more resistance than 1...g5 2 hxg5 Kxg5 3 Kf7 Kh5 4 Kf6) 2 Kf8! (not 2 Kf7? Kh7 holding the opposition) Kh5 3 Kg8! (again not 3 Kg7? f4!) Kh6 4 Kh8! Kh5 5 Kh7 g5 (or 5...f4 6 exf4 g5 7 f5! gxh4 8 f6 hxg3 9 f7 g2 10 f8/Q g1/Q 11 Qh6 mate) 6 hxg5 f4 7 gxf4 g3 8 g6 g2 9 g7 g1/Q 10 g8/Q and it's all over after a flurry of checks (10...Qb1+ 11 Kh8 Qa1+ 12 Qg7 Qa8+ 13 Kh7 Qe4+ 14 Kg8! Qa8+ 15 Qf8 Qg2+ 16 Kh8 Qb2+ 17 Qg7 Qb8+ 18 Kh7 Qb1+ 19 Kg8 Qb8+ 20 Qf8 Qb3+ 21 Qf7+ Qxf7 22 Kxf7 with two extra pawns).

19. B is the correct answer.
Choices: (a) Kg4 (b) f5+ (c) h4

(a) Black is really a pawn down because his doubled pawns count as one, but White is stymied after 1 Kg4? f5+ 2 Kh4 Kh6.

(b) White sacrifices to create an outside passed pawn and make space to penetrate with his king by 1 f5+! Kxf5 (if 1...Kg5 2 f6!) 2 h4 Ke5 (or 2...Kg6 3 Kg4 Kh6 4 h5) 3 Kg4 f6 4 h5 Ke6 5 h6 Kf7 6 Kf5 and wins.

(c) White can make no further progress after 1 h4? Kh5 2 Kg3 f5.

20. B is the correct answer.
Choices: (a) f4 (b) f6 (c) g5

(a) In the actual game White resigned after 1 f4? f6 3 g5 Kd4.

(b) White missed a win by 1 f6! gxf6 2 f4 Kd4 3 g5! fxg5 5 fxg5 Ke5 6 gxh6 Kf6 7 Kc2 and the h-pawn will queen after Black's king abandons f6.

(c) What a difference a move makes! 1 g5? f6! (of course not 1...hxg5? 2 f6 gxf6 3 h6) stops White cold.

21. C is the correct answer.
Choices: (a) g4 (b) f4 (c) h3

(a) The game continued 1 g4? fxg4! (but Black lost by 1...f4+ 2 Ke4 h6 3 h4 Kb6 4 g5 fxg5 5 hxg5 hxg5 6 Kxe5 g4 7 Kxf4 gxf3 8 Kxf3 Kc7 9 Ke4 Kd6 10 Kf5) 2 fxg4 h6 3 h4 Kb6 4 Ke4 Kc7 5 g5 fxg5 6 hxg5 hxg5 7 Kxe5 g4 8 Kf4 Kd6 9 Kxg4 Ke5=.

(b) White's king has no point of entry after 1 f4? h5=.

(c) The subtle 1 h3! h5 (if 1...Kb6 2 g4 fxg4 3 hxg4 followed by Ke4-f5 wins) 2 g4 fxg4 3 fxg4 hxg4 4 h4! wins because this passed pawn can't be stopped.

22. A is the correct answer.
Choices: (a) Kd3 (b) Kd4 (c) Kb4

(a) After 1 Kd3! Kd7 2 e4! f4 3 Ke2 Ke6 4 Kf2! Kxe5 5 Kf3 Black resigned because he is in zugzwang. Also 1 e4! f4 2 Kd2 Ke6 3 Ke2 Kxe5 4 Kf3 transposes into the winning line.

(b) A race to queen leads to a draw after 1 Kd4? Ke6 2 Kc5 Kxe5 3 Kxb5 Ke4 4 Kxa4 Kxe3 5 b4 f4 6 b5 f3 7 b6 f2 8 b7 f1/Q 9 b8/Q Qc4+ 10 Qb4 Kd3! 11 Ka5 (if 11 Qxc4+ Kxc4 12 Ka5 Kc5=) Qc7+=.

(c) The same draw is reached via 1 Kb4? Ke6 2 Kxb5 Kxe5.

23. B is the correct answer.
Choices: (a) g4 (b) h4 (c) Ke4

(a) Black has time to drive out the intruder after 1 g4? Ke7 2 h4 g6+ 3 Ke4 Kd6.

(b) White can maintain his active king on f5 by 1 h4! Ke7 2 h5 Kf7 (if 2...h6 3 Ke4! as in "c") 3 Ke4 Ke6 4 f5+ Kd6 5 Kd3! and Black, in zugzwang, resigned in view of 5...Kd5 (or 5...Ke5 5 Kc4) 6 b3 Kd6 7 Kc4 Kc6 8 g3 h6 9 g4 Kc7 10 Kb5 Kb7 11 a5 bxa5 12 Kxc5 Ka6 13 Kc6.

(c) Too passive is 1 Ke4? Ke6 and White has made no progress.

24. C is the correct answer.
Choices: (a) a4 (b) Kxc6 (c) Kd4

(a) White queens first after 1 a4? e5 2 a5 e4 but it's only a draw.

(b) Inadequate is 1 Kxc6? Kf3! 2 Kd5 Kf4! 3 a4 (or 3 Ke6 Ke4 4 a4 Kd4 5 a5 Kc5 6 a6 Kb6 catching the pawn) e5 4 a5 e4 and once again White queens first but can't win.

(c) The paradoxical retreat 1 Kd4! is the only winning move! The most testing defense is 1...e5+ (if 1...Kf3 2 a4! Kf4 3 a5 e5+ 4 Kc3! wins; or 1...c5+ 2 Kxc5 Kg3 3 a4 e5 4 a5 e4 5 Kd4 Kf4 6 a6 e3 7 Kd3 Kf3 8 a7 e2 9 a1/Q WITH CHECK) 2 Kxe5 Ke3 3 a4 Kd3 4 a5 c5 5 a6 c4 6 a7 c3 7 a8/Q c2 8 Qd5+! Ke2 9 Qa2 Kd3 (a cute finish is 9...Kd1 10 Kd4! c1/Q 11 Kd3! and White is helpless despite his queen) 10 Qb2! Kd2 11 Kd4 Kd1 12 Kd3 c1/Q 13 Qe2 mate.

25. C is the correct answer.
Choices: (a) Kc5 (b) Kd6 (c) g3

(a) Black loses the battle for the opposition after 1...Kc5? 2 Kd3 g3 3 f3! (but 3 fxg3? g4 turns the tables) Kd6 4 Kxd4, etc.

(b) The same goes for 1...Kd6? 2 Kd3 g3 (too late)! 3 fxg3

Kc5 4 g4 (trebuchet — whoever moves loses — see introduction).

(c) Correct is 1...g3! 2 f3! (again 2 fxg3? Kc5 3 Kd3 g4 wins for Black) Kd6 3 Kc2 Kc6= and both sides are held at bay.

26. B is the correct answer.
Choices: (a) Kf7 (b) Kd6 (c) Ke6

(a) 1...Kf7? allows White to gain a vital tempo by 2 h4. Timman, a pawn down, thinking his position was hopeless anyway, resigned without continuing play!

(b) The right defense is 1...Kd6! 2 h4 Kxc6 3 f5 Kd6! (in his mind's eye Timman probably only saw 3...gxf5? 4 h5 Kd6 5 g6 hxg6 6 h6) 4 f6 Ke6 5 Kf3 Kd6 6 Ke4 Ke6 7 Kd4 Kd6 8 Kc4 Ke6 9 Kc5 Kd7 10 Kd5 Ke8! 11 Kc6 Kd8 12 f7 Ke7 13 Kxc7 Kxf7 14 Kd7 Kf8 15 Ke6 Ke8 16 Kf6 Kf8= holding the opposition.

(c) Black can't afford to lose a tempo by 1...Ke6? 2 h4! Kd5 (no better is 2...Kf5 5 Kf3) 3 f5! gxf5 4 h5 Ke6 (if 4...Ke5 5 h6 f4 6 g6 hxg6 7 h7 wins) 5 Kf3 Ke5 6 h6 Ke6 7 Kf4 and wins easily.

27. A is the correct answer.
Choices: (a) h4 (b) c5 (c) g4

(a) Black's plan is to swap all the kingside pawns and then penetrate with his king to the queenside, but it's not easy. Correct is 1...h4! 2 Kh3! Ke5! (the only way; if 2...hxg3 3 Kxg3 c5 4 Kg2 Kf4 5 Kf2 g4 5 fxg4 Kxg4 6 Kg2 holding the opposition because Black has used up his reserve tempo with c5) 3 f4+ (if 3 gxh4 gxh4 4 Kxh4 Kf4) gxf4 4 gxh4 Ke4 5 Kg2 (if 5 h5 f3 6 h6 Ke3! 7 h7 f2 8 h8/Q f1/Q+ 9 Kg4 Qf4+ 10 Kh3 Kf2! wins) Kd3! 6 Kf3 Kxc3 7 h5 Kb3 8 h6 c3 9 h7 c2 10 h8/Q c1/Q with a winning queen and pawn ending.

(b) As seen in the previous variation 1...c5? is wrong because Black needs this reserve tempo in hand to gain the opposition later.

(c) Inadequate is 1...g4? 2 f4 h4 3 gxh4 (but not 3 Kg2 hxg3 4 Kxg3 c5! 5 Kg2 Kxf4) Kxf4 4 Kg2.

28. C is the correct answer.
Choices: (a) axb5 (b) cxb5 (c) d5+

(a) Two moves lose — one wins! Not 1...axb5? 2 c5! dxc5 3 dxc5 bxc5 4 a5 c4 5 a6 c3 6 Kd3 and Black can resign.

(b) Equally wrong is 1...cxb5? 2 a5! bxa5 3 c5 dxc5 4 bxc5 a4 5 c6 a3 (or 5...Ke7 6 f6+ Kxf6 7 c7) 6 c7 a2 7 c8/Q a1/Q 8 Qf8 mate!

(c) The game was adjudicated a win for Black in view of the surprising 1...d5+! 2 cxd5 (if 2 Ke3 cxb5! 3 c5 bxc5 4 dxc5 Kxf5 5 c6 Ke6 gets back in time) cxd5+ 3 Kxd5 axb5 4 Kc6 (a desperate attempt to avoid 4 axb5 g4 5 hxg4 hxg4 6 Ke4 g3 7 Kf3 Kxf5 8 Kxg3 Ke4) g4! 5 hxg4 h4! 6 d5 h3 7 d6 h2 8 d7 h1/Q queening first WITH CHECK.

29. B is the correct answer.
Choices: (a) h6 (b) Kc8 (c) a5

(a) Black lost after 1...h6? 2 h4! h5 (forced to stop h5 but now Black no longer has g5 at his disposal) 3 Kd5 Kd7 4 Kxe4 Kxd6 5 Kd4 Kc6 6 e4 and wins.

(b) Black can draw with the pawn still on h7: 1...Kc8! 2 h4 Kd8 3 Kd5 Kd7 4 Kxe4 Kxd6 5 Kd4 Ke6 6 e4 Kd6 7 Kc4 Kc6 8 Kb4 Kb6 9 Ka4 Kc5! 10 Ka5 Kd4 11 e5 Kd5 12 Ka6 Ke6 13 Kxa7 h6 14 Kb6 g5! 15 hxg5 hxg5 16 fxg5 Kxe5=.

(c) On 1...a5? 2 Kb5! (2 Kd5? Kd7 transposes into "b") Kd7 3 Kxa5 Kxd6 3 Kb4 Kd5 4 Kb5 h6 5 h4 h5 6. Kb4 Ke6 7 Kc4 Kf5 8 Kd4 Kg4 9 Kxe4 Kxh4 10 Kf3 g5 11 e4 g4+ 12 Kg2 g3 13 e5 wins.

30. A is the correct answer.
Choices: (a) d4 (b) c3 (c) Kg7

(a) After 1...d4! 2 e6 Kg7 3 f4 Kf6 4 f5 d3 5 Kb2 h5 White resigned because the pawns are unstoppable after 6 Kc1 b3! 7 a4 (if 7 axb3 cxb3 White is in zugzwang) c3.

(b) Premature is 1...c3? 2 Kb1 d4 3 Kc2 Kg7 4 f4 Kf7 5 f5=.

(c) Inaccurate is 1...Kg7? 2 a4! bxa3 3 Ka2 d4 4 Kxa3 d3 5 Kb2 Kg6 6 f4=.

31. B is the correct answer.
Choices: (a) c5 (b) a5 (c) Ke7

(a) The game continued 1...c5? 2 Ke3! and a draw was agreed because if 2...Ke7 3 f4! exf4+ 4 Kxf4. White dashes his king to the queenside while Black's king is tethered to the kingside .

(b) By creating an outside passed pawn Black can prevent White from getting rid of his weak doubled pawns: 1...a5! 2 Kd3 (no time for 2 Ke3 b4 3 f4 exf4+ 4 Kxf4 a4! 5 Ke3 b3 6 axb3 a3 and White's king is outside the square to stop this pawn) a4 3 Kc3 c5 4 g4 Ke7 5 Kd3 Ke6 6 Kc3 Kd5 7 a3 Ke6 8 Kd3 Kd6 9 Kc3 Kd5 10 Kd3 b4 11 axb4 cxb4 12 Kc2 Kc4 13 Kb2 a3+ 14 Ka2 Kc3 wins.

(c) The drawback to 1...Ke7? is that White has time for 2 Ke3 Ke6 3 f4! exf4 4 Kxf4 dissolving the weakness before steering his king to the queenside.

32. C is the correct answer.
Choices: (a) f3 (b) h5 (c) b6

(a) Black lost after 1...f3? 2 gxf3 gxf3 3 c5 Kd5 4 c6 bxc6 5 b6 axb6 6 a6!

(b) The same fate befalls 1...h5? 2 c5 Kd5 3 c6! bxc6 4 b6! axb6 5 a6.

(c) An elementary precaution wins by 1...b6! 2 axb6 (or 2 c5 bxa5!) axb6 3 c5 bxc5 4 b6 Kd6 5 b7 Kc7 6 b8/Q+ Kxb8 7 Ke4 Kc7 8 Kxf4 h5 9 h3 c4!

33. C is the correct answer.
Choices: (a) dxc4 (b) a5 (c) Kf5

(a) Black lost after the careless 1...dxc4? 2 h4 a5 3 h5 a4 4 h6 gxh6 5 d5+ Kf6 6 d6 a3 7 d7 Ke7 8 g7 a2 9 g8/Q a1/Q 10 d8/Q mate.

(b) Black also loses after 1...a5? 2 h4 a4 3 cxd5+ Kxd5 4 Kd3 a3 5 Kc3 a2 6 Kb2 Kxd4 7 h5 Ke5 8 h6 Kf6 9 h7!

(c) A simple path to victory is 1...Kf5! 2 cxd5 Kxg6 followed by Kf7-e7-d6.

34. C is the correct answer.
Choices: (a) Kd7 (b) Kf6 (c) Kf7

(a) Repeating the position by 1...Kd7 2 Ke5 Ke7 leads nowhere.

(b) Black wants to play 1...g5 but not immediately because of 2 hxg5 Kf7 3 Ke5 Kg6 4 Kf4. And if 1...Kf6? 2 Kc6 g5 3 hxg5+ (this check is crucial because it gains time when Black recaptures) Kxg5 3 Kxb6 h4 neither side can win after they both queen.

(c) The point behind 1...Kf7! is to play g5 at the proper moment . On 2 Kc6 (or 2 Ke5 Kg7 3 Ke4 Kf6 4 Kf4 g5+! 5 hxg5+ Kg6 and White lands in zugzwang) g5 3 Kxb6 (if 3 hxg5 h4 queens too fast) gxh4 4 Kc5 (any other square permits a decisive queen swap; e.g., 4 Kc7 h3 5 b6 h2 6 b7 h1/Q 7 b8/Q Qh2+ and Qxb8) Ke7! 5 b6 Kd7 stopping the pawn, whereas White cannot do the same.

35. B is the correct answer.
Choices: (a) a5 (b) Kc6 (b) (c) a6

(a) Black lost after 1...a5? 2 Kf5 Kd6 3 Kg5 Ke5 4 f3! Ke6 5 f4 h4 6 Kxh4 Kf6 7 Kg4 Kg6 8 Kf3 Kf6 9 Ke4 Ke6 10 Kd4!

(b) Black can draw by 1...Kc6! 2 Kf5 (or 2 a5 h4 3 Kf4 Kd5 7 Kg4 Ke4! 8 Kxh4 Kf3) Ke5 3 Kg5 Ke4! 4 f4 h4.

(c) Too slow is 1...a6? 2 Kf5 Kd6 (or 2...h4 3 Kf4 Kd6 4 Kg4 Ke5 5 a5) 3 Kg5 Ke5 4 f4+! Ke6 5 a5.

36. C is the correct answer.
Choices: (a) Kb6 (b) Kd6 (c) Kd7

(a) Shun 1...Kb6? 2 Kd5 and Black is hard-pressed to find a good move.

(b) Black ends up a pawn down in a difficult queen ending after 1...Kd6 2 f4 Kc6 3 b4! cxb4 4 Kxb4 Kb6 5 a5+ Kc6 6 Kc4 Kd6 7 Kd4 Ke6 8 Kc5 Kf5 9 Kb6 Kxf4 10 Kxa6 g5 11 hxg5 h4 12 g6 h3 13 g7 h2 14 g8/Q h1/Q 15 Qc4.

(c) Black drew by 1...Kd7! 2 f4 (more prudent than 2 Kd5? g5! 3 hxg5 h4 4 g6 Ke7 and Black wins! but 2 Kxc5 g5 3 Kd4! draws) Kd6 3 Kd3 a5 4 Kc4 Kc6=.

37. B is the correct answer.
Choices: (a) h6 (b) Kb5 (c) Kb6

(a) As we have seen, it's foolish to use up a reserve tempo if it can come in handy later to wrest the opposition. After 1...h6? 2 Kd3 Kb5 3 a4+ Kb6 (the king lands out of the square on 3...Kxa4? 4 d6) 4 Kc4 a5 5 Kd3 Kc7 6 Kc3 Kd7=.

(b) Black is a pawn up and won with 1...Kb5! (threatening c4) 2 a4+ Kb6 3 Kc4 a5 4 d6 (also hopeless is 4 Kc3 Kc7 5 Kd3 Kd6 6 Kc4 h6! when the reserve tempo decides) Kc6 5 d7 Kxd7 6 Kxc5 Ke7 7 Kd5 (the king must rush to the kingside since 7 Kb5 h5! wins) Kf7 8 Ke4 Kf8! 9 Ke3 Ke7! 10 Ke4 Kd6 11 Kd4 h6 12 Ke4 Kc5 13 Ke3 Kd5 14 Kd3 Ke5 15 Ke3 h5 (finally!) 16 gxh5 Kxf5 17 Kf3 Ke6 18 Kg4 Kf7 19 Kf5 Kg7.

(c) A draw ensues on 1...Kb6? 2 Kc4 a5 3 a4 h6 (Black uses up his precious tempo to force a retreat) 4 Kc3 Kc7 5 Kd3 Kd7=.

38. B is the correct answer.
Choices: (a) a5 (b) a6 (c) Kf6

(a) Black lost after 1...a5? 2 g3 h5+ 3 Kh4 Kh6 4 g4 hxg4 5 Kxg4 Kg6 6 Kf4 Kf6 7 b3! (finally using the reserve tempo decisively) Ke6 8 Kg5 penetrating.

(b) Black has a surprising draw by 1...a6! 2 b4 b5 3 a5 Kf6 4 Kh5 Kf5! (clearly hopeless is 4...Kg7? 5 g4 Kh7 6 g5) 5 Kxh6 Kf4 6 g3+ Kf3! (not 6...Kxg3? Kg5) 7 Kh5 Ke4! 8 g4 Kxd4 9 g5 Kc3 10 g6 d4 11 g7 d3 12 g8/Q d2 and White can't win because c4 is inacessible to his queen!

(c) Feeble resistance is offered by 1...Kf6? 2 Kh5 Kg7 3 g4 Kh7 4 g5 hxg5 5 Kxg5 Kg7 6 Kf5 Kf7 7 Ke5 followed by Kxd5.

39. B is the correct answer.
Choices: (a) Kf2 (b) Kg3 (c) g6

(a) Black let the win slip away by 1...Kf2? 2 f5! Kg2 (if 2...Kg3 3 Ke3! Kg4 4 Ke4 keeps the opposition) 3 Kf4 Kf2 (but not 3...Kh3? 4 Kg5 Kg3 9 f6!) 4 Ke4 Kg2=.

(b) Correct is 1...Kg3! 2 Ke3 g6 3 Ke4 Kf2 4 f5 gxf5+ 5 Kxf5 Ke3 and Black gets to the queenside "fustest with the mostest."

(c) Hideous is 1...g6?? 2 f5! gxf5+ 3 Kxf5 Kf3 4 Ke5 and White wins.

40. A is the correct answer.
Choices: (a) Kb5 (b) Kd5 (c) Kd3

(a) The only drawing move is 1...Kb5! 2 Kb3 c4!+ 3 Kc2 Kc5 4 Kd2 Kd5 5 Ke3 Ke5 when neither king can penetrate.

(b) Fatal is 1...Kd5? 2 Kb3 Kd6 3 Ka4 Kc6 4 Ka5 Kd5 5 Kb5 Kd6 6 c4.

(c) Equally lugubrious is 1...Kd3? 2 Kb3 Ke4 3 Kc4 Kf5 4 Kxc5 Kg5 5 Kd6 Kxh5 6 c4 Kxg6 7 c5 and the pawn queens too fast.

41. C is the correct answer.
Choices: (a) Ke5 (b) Ke7 (c) f4

(a) The natural 1...Ke5? loses to 2 Kd7 Ke4 3 Ke6 Kxe3 (or 3...Kf3 4 Kxf6! Kxg3 5 Kxf5 Kxh4 6 Kf4! Kh3 7 e4) 4 Kxf5! Kf3 5 Kxf6 Kxg3 6 Kg5.

(b) 1...Ke7? 2 Kc7 Ke6 3 Kd8 Ke5 4 Ke7 leads to the same fate.

(c) A process of elimination shows that Black's only hope is 1...f4! 2 gxf4 Kf5 3 Kd5 Kg4 4 Ke6 Kxh4 5 Kxf6 Kg4 6 e4 h4=.

42. A is the correct answer.
Choices: (a) Kg4 (b) Kf4 (c) Ke4

(a) A pawn down on an open board, it is hard to believe that stalemate is White's saving resource: 1 Kg4 Kd7 2 Kf5! (not 2 Kh5? Ke6 3 Kh6 Kf5) Ke8 (if 2...d5 3 Ke5 e6 4 Kf6) 3 Ke6 Kf8 4 d3! Ke8 5 d4 Kd8 6 d5 Ke8 7 g6! hxg6=.

(b) White can't afford to lose a tempo by 1 Kf4? Kc6 2 Kf5 Kd5 with an active king instead of being forced back to the first rank (as in "a").

(c) The same goes for 1 Ke4? Kc6 2 Kf5 Kd5.

43. A is the correct answer.
Choices: (a) Kc5 (b) Kc3 (c) Kc4

(a) 1 Kc5! Kg6 (no better is 1...g5 2 b4 g4 3 Kd4! Kg5 4 b6 g3 5 Ke3 Kg4 6 b6 Kh3 7 b7 g2 8 Kf2 Kh2 9 b8/Q+) 2 b4 Kf7 3

10 Ke5 Kxh4 11 Kf4 Kh3 12 e4 Kg2 13 e5! h4 14 e6 winning as shown above.

(b) If 1 Kg2 Ke4 2 Kf2 Kf4! draws. White could win here were Black on move!

(c) Black holds against 1 Kh2 Kd4! 2 Kg2 Ke4! 3 Kf2 Kf4= and again White finds himself on the move and thus can make no progress (4 Kf1 Kg4).

49. B is the correct answer.
Choices: (a) Kg2 (b) g4 (c) Kh3

(a) White perishes after 1 Kg2? Kh7 2 Kf3 Kh6 3 Ke4 Kg5 4 Kxe5 Kg4 5 Ke6 Kxg3 6 Kf7 Kg4.

(b) A pawn down, White must fight for a draw by 1 g4! hxg4 (or 1...Kh7 2 g5! g6 3 f6 Kg8 4 Kg3 Kf7 5 Kf3 Ke6 6 Kg3=) 2 Kg3 Kh7 3 Kh4! (not 3 Kxg4? Kh6 4 Kh4 e4 5 Kg3 e3) Kh8 4 Kxg4 Kg8 5 Kh4! Kf7 6 Kg5 and Black can't utilize his extra pawn.

(c) Inadequate is 1 Kh3? e4! 2 Kg2 Kh7 3 Kf2 Kh6 4 Ke3 Kg5 5 Kxe4 Kg4 transposing into "a."

50. A is the correct answer.
Choices: (a) b5 (b) h3 (c) a5

(a) White created a deadly passed pawn with 1 b5! Kh5 (no better is 1...Kf6 2 Kg4 g5 3 Kh5) 2 a5! bxa5 3 b6! cxd6 4 d6 and this foot soldier marches to glory.

(b) White also wins but it takes longer after 1 h3 b5! 2 axb5 b6 3 Ke3 Kf6 4 f4 g5 5 f5 Kf7 6 Kf3 Kg7 7 Kg4 Kh6 8 f6 Kg6 9 f7 Kxf7 10 Kxg5, etc.

(c) Black wrests the advantage after 1 a5? bxa5 2 bxa5 Kh5 3. h3 g5.

51. B is the correct answer.

Choices: (a) Kf7 (b) Re4 (c) Re5

(a) The Lucena position, discovered over 500 years ago, is akin to the Rosetta stone of chess. This type of ending with the pawn on its seventh rank has occurred countless times. White merely goes around in circles after 1 Kf7 Rf2+ 2 Kg6 Rg2+ 3 Kh7 Rh2+ 4 Kg8 Rg2.

(b) The key to victory is shielding the king from incessant checks by "building a bridge" with 1 Re4! Rh1 2 Kf7 Rf1+ 3 Kg6 Rg1+ 4 Kf6 Rf1+ 5 Kg5 Rg1+ 6 Rg4! Rxg4+ 7 Kxg4 and the pawn queens.

(c) Less accurate is 1 Re5 Kd6 2 Kf7? (2 Re4! gets back to a simpler win) Rf2+ 3 Ke8 Kxe5 4 g8/Q leading to a long queen vs. rook ending that requires technical expertise to win (see diagram 101).

52. A is the correct answer.
Choices: (a) Ra3 (b) Rf7+ (c) Kf1

(a) In the late 18th century Andre Philidor showed that the easiest way to draw this basic ending is to keep White's rook on the third rank to prevent the king from penetrating and then going to the eighth rank after the pawn pushes. Thus 1 Ra3! e3 (or 1...Rb2 2 Rc3 waiting) 2 Ra8! and Black can make no progress.

(b) White can still draw after 1 Rf7+ Ke3 2 Kf1 but makes it hard for himself.

(c) The same goes for 1 Kf1 Kf3 2 Rf7+ Ke3 (see diagram 53).

53. C is the correct answer.
Choices: (a) Rf1 (b) Kd1 (c) Kf1

(a) It's easy to dispose of 1 Rf1? 2 Ra2 followed by Ra1+.

(b) Also bad is 1 Kd1? Rh1+ 2 Kc2 Ke2 ushering the pawn home.

(c) The best defense is going to the short side by 1 Kf1! Rh1+ 2 Kg2 Re1 3 Ra8! Rd1 4 Re8! Kd3 5 Kf2 preventing White from freeing his king by Ke2. (Also see diagram 98.)

54. B is the correct answer.
Choices: (a) d7 (b) Rh8 (c) Rg8

(a) A tasty trap is 1 d7? Re6+ 2 Kf7 Rf6+! (but not 2...Kd6? 3 Re8!) 3 Kg7 Ke6 4 Re8+ Kxd7 5 Kxf6 Kxe8 and it's down to bare knuckles.

(b) In general a rook should stay as far away as possible when planning checks on an open board. A simple win is 1 Rh8! Rxd6 2 Rh5+ Kf4 Kxd6.

(c) White throws away the win by 1 Rg8? Rxd6 2 Rg5+ Kf4 3 Kxd6 Kxg5=.

55. B is the correct answer.
Choices: (a) Kc5 (b) Kb5 (c) Kb7

(a) It's a draw after 1 Kc5? Rd1 2 Kc6 (the rash 2 c8/Q? Rc1+ and Rxc8 wins for Black!) Rc1+ 3 Kb7=.

(b) This famous study is sometimes called the Saavedra position because a monk by that name first discovered the underpromotion on move 5. The actual game was drawn but White missed a splendid win by 1 Kb5! Rd5+ 2 Kb4 Rd4+ 3 Kb3 Rd3+ 4 Kc2 Rd5! (hoping for 5 c8/Q? Rc5+ 6 Qxc5 stalemate) 5 c8/R! Ra5 (necessary to stop 6 Ra8) 6 Kb3! and White either mates or captures the rook. (A similar trick is seen in the solution to diagram 56.)

(c) If 1 Kb7? Rd7 draws by pinning the pawn and then giving up the rook to stop it from queening.

56. B is the correct answer.
Choices: (a) exf5 (b) Rg1+ (c) Rxf5

(a) The insipid 1 exf5? Ra7+ 2 Kf6 Ra6+ 3 Kg5 Kf7= reaches the Philidor position (see diagram 52).

(b) An incredible pawn sacrifice lures Black's rook to a fatal square: 1 Rg1+ Kh7 2 e5! (not a typo!) Rxe5+ (or 2...f4 3 e6 f3 4 Kf6! f2 5 Rf1 Kg8 6 Rxf2 Kf8 7 Rb2 Ra8 8 Rh2 Kg8 9 Rg2+ Kf8 10 e7+ also wins) 3 Kf7 Kh6 4 Kf6 threatening Rh1 mate and/or Kxe5. Chessboard magic!

(c) Insufficient is 1 Rxf5? Ra7+ 2 Kd6 Ra6+ 3 Ke5 Ra5+ 4 Kf4 Rxf5+ 5 Kxf5 Kf7 6 Ke5 Ke7= (Black has the opposition).

57. A is the correct answer.
Choices: (a) Ke4 (b Ke2 (c) Rc2

(a) White wants to cross over to the queenside with his king to blockade the pawn but it can't be done, so his best defense is to shuffle from e4 to e3 while trying to restrain the forward march of the pawn. Thus 1 Ke4! Rd4+ 2 Ke3 Kb5 3 Rb1+ Kc4 (if 3...Rb4 4 Rc1 c4 5 Kd4) 4 Rc1+ Kb4 5 Rb1+ Ka4 6 Rc1! Rd5 7 Ke4! Rh5 8 Kd3!=.

(b) White lost after 1 Ke2? Kb5 2 Rb1+ Ka4 3 Rc1 Kb4 4 Rb1+ Ka3 5 Rc1 Rd5! and now Ke4 is no longer possible because the king is on e2.

(c) There's no single rule to govern these positions because the outcome often depends on one tempo, yet an important principle is to keep the rook far away from the enemy king when checking: 1 Rc2? (violates this principle) Kb4 2 Rb2+ (or 2 Rd2 Rxd2 3 Kxd2 Kb4! 4 Kc2 Kc4 seizing the opposition wins) Kc4 3 Rc2+ Kb4 4 Rb2+ Kc3 followed by c4 wins.

58. C is the correct answer.
Choices: (a) Kf7 (b) Kd7 (c) Ra5

(a) Black checks to his heart's content after 1 Kf7? Rf1+ 2 Kg7 (if 2 Ke8 Rf2!=) Rg1+ , etc.

(b) Going the other way also provides no shelter after 1 Kd7 Rd1+ 2 Kc7 Rc1+.

(c) Black gets in zugzwang after 1 Ra5! Kg4 (or 1...Kh3 2 Ra4!) 2 Kf7! Rf1+ 3 Kg6 Re1 (3...a1/Q 4 Rxa1 Rxa1 5 e8/Q leads to a theoretical queen vs. rook win — see diagram 101) 4 Ra4+ Kh3 5 Kf6 Rf1+ 6 Kg5 Rg1+ 7 Kh5 Re1 8 Ra3+! Kg2 9 Rxa3+ Kf3 10 Ra7 Re6! (the toughest defense) 11 Kg5 Ke4 12 Rb7! (but not the obvious 12 Rd7? Ke5! when White is in zugzwang) Ke5 13 Rd7! Ke4 14 Rd1! Kf3 (14...Rxe7 15 Re1+ and Rxe7 costs the rook) 15 Rf1+ Ke2 16 Rf7 Ke3 17 Kf5 wins. Whew!

59. B is the correct answer.
Choices: (a) Rh5+ (b) Kb7 (c) Kd8

(a) Black's king is driven to a better position after 1 Rh5+? Kb6 2 Rh6+ Ka7=.

(b) A curious stepping maneuver leads to a queen vs. rook finale: 1 Kb7! Rb2+ 2 Ka7 Rc2 3 Rh5+ Ka4 (the king is forced back) 4 Kb7 Rb2+ 5 Ka6 Rc2 6 Rh4+ Ka3 7 Kb6 Rb2+ (White was threatening Rxh2) 8 Ka5! Rc2 9 Rh3+ Ka2 10 Rxh2! Rxh2 11 c8/Q.

(c) A loss of time is 1 Kd8 Rd2+ 2 Ke8 Re2+ but White can still find the winning idea with 3 Kd7 Rd2+ 4 Kc6 Rc2+ 5 Kb7 Rb2+ 6 Ka7 Rc2 7 Rh5+ as in "a". (See diagram 58 for a variation on this theme.)

60. B is the correct answer.
Choices: (a) b4 (b) Rh5+ (c) Rd3

(a) Premature is 1 b4? Rc8+ 2 Kb5 Rb8+ 3 Ka4 Ra8+ 4 Kb3 Kd6=.

(b) White's king must stay active while keeping Black's king cut off from the queenside by 1 Rh5+! Ke6 2 Rh6+ Kd7 3 Rh7+ Ke6 4 b4! Rc8+ 5 Kb6 Rb8+ 6 Rb7 Rh8 7 b5 and wins.

(c) Little is achieved by 1 Rd3 Ke4 2 Rd4+ (2 Rh3 Ke5 repeats the position) Ke5 3 Rb4 Rc8+ 4 Kb5 Rb8+ 5 Kc4 Rc8+ 6 Kd3 Kd6 getting the king in front of the pawn.

61. C is the correct answer.
Choices: (a) Kd2 (b) Rh8 (c) Rf8+

(a) The king can't get to the kingside in view of 1 Kd2? h3 2 Ke2 h2 3 Rh8 Ra1! 4 Rxh2 Ra2+ and Rxh2 (this tactic is known as an x-ray).

(b) White lost quickly with 1 Rh8? h3 2 Kb2 (or 2 Kd2 h2 wins) Kg3! 3 Rg8+ Kh2 followed by Rg1.

(c) The correct defense is 1 Rf8+! Kg3 (if 1...Kg5 2 Rg8+ Kh6 3 Kb2! h3 4 Rg3! Kh5 5 Rc3!=) 2 Rg8+ Kh2 3 Kd2 h3 4 Ke2 Rg1 5 Rh8 Kg2 6 Rg8+ Kh1 7 Rh8 h2 8 Kf2 locking Black's king in the corner.

62. A is the correct answer.
Choices: (a) b6 (b) Rh8 (c) Ke4

(a) White won by 1 b6! cxb6 (or 1...Kc6 1 Rb8) 2 Rh8 Rxa7 3 Rh7+ winning the rook (another x-ray attack). Note that Black would draw if his king stood on g7 or h7.

(b) An easy draw follows 1 Rh8? Rxa7 2 Rxh6.

(c) Superfluous is 1 Ke4 h5 but 2 b6! still wins.

63. C is the correct answer.
Choices: (a) Kxf5 (b) Kg5 (c) Rf8

(a) The pawn is poisoned! Almost any move wins except 1 Kxf5? Rxf2+ 2 Kxg4 Ra2 and White can't make progress despite two extra pawns because his rook is entombed as long as Black shuttles his king between g7 and h7. Any attempt by White's king to approach the queenside is foiled by checks from behind.

(b) A longwinded victory is possible 1 Kg5 Kg7 2 Rb8 Rxa7 3 Rb5 Ra6 4 Rxf5 Rg6+ 5 Kh4.

(c) The sharpest method is 1 Rf8! Rxa7 2 Rf7+ Rxf7 3 Kxf7 f4 4 gxf4 Kh6 5 f5 Kg5 6 f6 Kf4 7 Kg6 Kf3 8 Kg5 and Black resigned.

64. C is the correct answer.
Choices: (a) Rd2 (b) f3 (c) Kg3

(a) It took some doing, but White lost after 1 Rd2? Kh4 2 Kxf5 g3 3 f4 (Geller saw a mirage thinking he could play fxg3+ which is illegal!) Ra1 4 Ke5? (the final indignity; 4 Rd8! g2 5 Rh8+ Kg3 6 Rg8+ Kf3 7 Ke6! still would draw) Kg4 5 f5 Ra5+ and White resigned.

(b) White transforms himself into a pin cushion after 1 f3? Kh4 2 Ra3 Kh3 3 Rb3 Rf2 4 Ra3 Kg2 5 Kxf5 Rxf3+ 6 Rxf3 gxf3 and the pawn queens.

(c) Two pawns vs. one on the same side usually draw. It's hard to see how Black makes progress on 1 Kg3 Kg5 2 Rd5.

65. A is the correct answer.
Choices: (a) Rc8+ (b) Rxd6 (c) Rc7

(a) The solution is 1 Rc8+ Kxc8 2 b7+ Kb8 3 d5 Kc7 (zugzwang) 4 bxa8/B! (only this underpromotion wins!) Kb8 5 Bb7 Kc7 6 Kxa7, etc.

(b) Black draws easily on 1 Rxd6? axb6+ 2 Kxb6 Ra7.

(c) It's a draw after 1 Rc7? axb6+ 2 Kxb6 Ra6+ 3 Kxa6 Kxc7=.

66. C is the correct answer.
Choices: (a) Rxa4 (b) Kxf6+ (c) Ra8

(a) White has no good follow-up after 1 Rxa4? Rxg6=.

(b) On 1 Kxf6+? Kh6 2 Rh5+ Kxh5 3 Kxg7 a3 4 Kf7 a2 5 g7 it peters out into a draw after both sides queen.

(c) Material superiority does not always confer an advantage! Here White is a pawn down yet wins because Black is in a mating net: 1 Ra8! Rxg6 2 Rh8+ Rh6 3 Rg8! Kh4 (if 3...Rh7 4 Rg1 Kh6 5 Kxf6 Kh5 6 Rh1+ nets a rook; or 3...a3 4 Rg1 Kh4 5 Rh1+ Kg3 6 Rxh6 a2 7 Rh1 wins) 4 Rg1 Rh5+ 5 Kf4! Kh3 6 Rh1+ Kg2 7 Rxh5 does the trick.

67. C is the correct answer.
Choices: (a) Rf1 (b) Rg1 (c) Kd2

(a) It's only a draw after 1 Rf1? g2 2 Ke1! gxf1/Q+ 3 Kxf1.

(b) White loses because the pawns are so liquid after 1 Rg1? f2 2 Rf1 g2 3 Ke2 g1/Q! 4 Rxf2 Ke5. (See diagram 101 for how a queen beats a rook.)

(c) The trick is a discovered check after 1 Kd2! f2 (or 1...g2 2 Ke3) 2 Rd1! g2 3 Ke2+ Ke5 4 Kxf2 picking up both pawns.

68. C is the correct answer.
Choices: (a) f7 (b) Ke5 (c) g7

(a) Too hasty is 1 f7? Rxg6+ 2 Ke5 (if 2 Ke7 Rg7 pins the pawn and draws) Rg5+! 3 Ke4 Rg1! and White now must go for the draw with 4 Ke5 since 4 f8/Q? Re1+ 5 Kf5 Rf1+ and Rxf8 wins.

(b) 1 Ke5? Rxg6 2 f7 Rg5+! transposes into the draw as in "a".

(c) Two advanced, connected passed pawns usually defeat

a rook when they are supported by a king if the opposing king is far away — but care must be exercised. The quietus is 1 g7! Kd4 2 Kc6!! (theatening f7; but neither 2 f7? Rg6+ 3 Ke7 Rxg7 nor 2 Ke6? Ke4! 3 Kf7 Ke5 4 g8/Q Rxg8 5 Kxg8 Kxf6 force a win) Kc4 3 Kd7! (not 3 Kb6? Rg6! 4 Ka5 Rg5+ 5 Ka4 Rg1 6 Ka3 Kc3 7 Ka2 Rg2+ etc.) Kd5 4 Ke8 Ke6 5 f7 Ra1 6 f8/N+! (underpromotion) Kd6 7 g8/Q.

69. B is the correct answer.
Choices: (a) Rh4 (b) Rd2 (c) Rd1

(a) After 1 Rh4? d4 2 Kd7 d3 3 Kc6 d2 4 Rh1 Kd4 5 Kb5 Kd3 6 Kb4 Kc2=. Black will have to give up his rook for the pawn.

(b) The winning theme is to lose a move to gain the opposition: 1 Rd2! d4 2 Rd1! Kd5 (or 2...Ke4 3 Kd6 d3 4 Kc5 Ke3 6 Kc4 d2 7 Kc3 catching the pawn) 3 Kd7! (not 3 Kf6? Ke4 4 Ke6 d3 and Black snatches the opposition) Kc4 4 Ke6 d3 5 Ke5 Kc3 6 Ke4 d2 7 Ke3 nabbing the upstart from the other side.

(c) The natural retreat only draws: 1 Rd1? d4 2 Kd7 Kd5! 3 Kc7 Kc5! 4 Kb7 Kc4 5 Kc6 d3 and the pawn supported by the king will soon compel Black to give up his rook for the pawn.

70. C is the correct answer.
Choices: (a) f7 (b) Kg7 (c) Kf7

(a) Careless is 1 f7? b4 2 Kg7 b3 3 f8/Q Rxf8 4 Kxf8 b2 5 g6 b1/Q 6 g7 Qb8+. A queen without the aid of its king can force a win against any enemy pawn on the seventh rank except a c-pawn or f-pawn.

(b) 1 Kg7? b4 2 f7 b3 transposes into the same win as “a”.

(c) The game continued 1 Kf7! b4 2 g6 b3 3 g7 b2 4 g8/Q b1/Q and a draw was agreed in view of 5 Qg6+ Kc3 6 Qxb1 Rxb1 7 Ke7 forcing Black to sacrifice his rook for the pawn.

71. B is the correct answer.
Choices: (a) Rc8+ (b) Rg8 (c) Rf8

(a) White must go after one of the pawns, but which one? For starters, eliminate moves which help the opponent improve his position such as 1 Rc8+? Kd4 2 Rb8 g3 3 Rxb5 g2 4 Rg5 f3 and the rook is helpless.

(b) This looks impossible but the solution is 1 Rg8! g3 (or 1...f3 2 Rxg4 b4 3 Rf4=) 2 Rg4 b4 3 Rxf4 b3 4 Rf1! g2 5 Rg1 b2 6 Kg7 Kd4 7 Kf6 Ke3 8 Rb1! Kd3 9 Rg1!=. When the king goes to the second rank, a pawn falls WITH CHECK.

(c) Plausible but wrong is 1 Rf8? f3 2 Rf4 b4 3 Rxg4 b3 4 Rg1 b2 5 Rb1 f2 6 Kg7 Kd4 7 Kf6 Kd3 8 Ke5 Kc2 9 Rf1 b1Q 10 Rxf2+ Kd3 and once again the queen triumphs over the rook. (See diagram 101.)

72. C is the correct answer.
Choices: (a) Rxh5+ (b) Kc3 (c) Rh8

(a) White must be content with a draw by perpetual check after 1 Rxh5+? Kd4 2 Rh8 (of course not 2 Kxa4 d2 and queens with check) Ra1 3 Rd8+ Ke3 4 Re8+ Kd4, etc.

(b) Also drawn is 1 Kc3? Ra3+ 2 Kd2 Kd4 3 Rxh5 Ra2+ 4 Ke1 Ke3 5 Re5+ Kf3 6 f5 Rxh2 7 f6 Kxg3 8 Rg5+ Kh4 9 f7 d2+ 10 Kd1 Rf2=.

(c) In general rooks belong BEHIND passed pawns. White won with 1 Rh8! Ra1 (if 1...Rd4 2 Rc8+ Kd5 3 Kc3! followed by Kd2) 2 Kc3 Ra3+ 3 Kd2 Ra2+ 4 Kxd3 Rxh2 5 Ke4 Rh3 6 Kf3.

73. B is the correct answer.
Choices: (a) Rc6+ (b) Rf1+ (c) Rf7

(a) Pointless is 1 Rc6+? Kd2 2 Rc7 Ke3 3 Rf7 Ke4 4 Kb1 Ke5 5 Kc1 Ke6 6 Ra7 Kf6 followed by Kg6 and the pawn falls.

(b) A theoretically won Queen vs. Rook ending is possible after 1 Rf1+! Kd2 2 Rf2+! Rxf2 3 h8/Q (see diagram 101).

(c) Too slow is 1 Rf7? Rh6 2 Ka2 Kd2= followed by a trek to g6 as in "a".

74. B is the correct answer.
Choices: (a) Kc6 (b) Rxh2 (c) a6

(a) The game was drawn because White lost a precious tempo with 1 Kc6? Rc1+ 2 Kb6 Rc4! 3 Rxh2 (if 3 b5 Rh4) Rxb4+ 4 Kc5 Ra4=.

(b) It's necessary to drag the king one square further away by 1 Rxh2! Kxh2 2 Ka6 Kg3 3 b5 Kf4 4 b6 Ke5 5 b7 Rb1 6 Ka7 Kd6 7 b8/Q+ Rxb8 8 Kxb8 Kc6 9 a6 and queens.

(c) Black gets back in the nick of time after 1 a6? h1/Q 2 Rxh1 Rxh1 3 a7 Ra1 4 Kb6 Kf4 5 Kb7 Ke5 6 b5 (or 6 a8/Q Rxa8 7 Kxa8 Kd5! 8 Ka7 Kc4=) Kd5 7 b6 Kc5 8 a8/Q Rxa8 9 Kxa8 Kxb5 and it's down to skin and bones.

75. A is the correct answer.
Choices: (a) Rb6 (b) Rc5 (c) Kb4

(a) Surprisingly, the only way to win is 1 Rb6! Rh5+ 2 Kb4 Rh4+ 3 Kc5 Rh5+ 4 Kd4 Rh4+ 5 Ke5 Rh5+ 6 Kf4 Rh4+ 7 Kg5 Rh8 8 Rc6! Kb8 (forced to meet the threat of Rc8) 9 Kg6 Rf8 10 Kg7 Rd8 11 Rf6 followed by Rf8.

(b) Ineffectual is 1 Rc5? Rh6! 2 Kb5 Rb6+ 3 Kc4 Rxa6=.

(c) White makes no headway by 1 Kb4 Rh4+ 2 Kc5 Rh5+ 3 Kd6 Rh6+ 4 Ke7 Rh8! (but not 4...Rh7+? 5 Kf6 Rh8 6 Rc5 Kxa6 7 Rc8 Rh6+ 8 Kg5 wins) and if 5 Rc5 Kxa6 6 Rc8 Rh7+ picks up the pawn.

76. B is the correct answer.
Choices: (a) Rg7 (b) Rg5 (c) Rg1+

(a) Black is winning after 1 Rg7? b2 2 Rxb7 b1/Q 3 Rxb1+ Kxb1 4 Kg3 Kc2 5 Kf3 Kd3 6 Kf2 Ke4 7 Kg3 Ke3 with a squeeze play.

(b) The decisive blow is so stunning it looks like a typographical error: 1 Rg5! hxg5 (Black must accept this Grecian gift, since 1...b2 2 Rxf5 b1/Q 3 Ra5+ Kb2 4 Rb5+ Kc2 5 Rxb1 Kxb1 f5 wins easily) 2 h6 b2 3 h7 b1/Q 4 h8/Q+ Qb2+ (or 4...Ka2 5 Qa8+ Kb2 6 Qxb7+ wins) 5 Qxb2+ Kxb2 6 fxg5 wins!

(c) If White doesn't win, he loses! Futile is 1 Rg1+? Ka2 2 Kg3 b2 3 Kf2 b1/Q 4 Rxb1 Kxb1 5 Ke3 Kc2 6 Kd4 b5.

77. A is the correct answer.
Choices: (a) Ra7+ (b) Rh6 (c) Kxh5

(a) White is two pawns down but it's hard to see how Black can break the blockade after 1 Ra7+! Kf8 2 Ra8+ Kf7 3 Ra7+ Kg6 4 Ra6+ Kf5 (or 4...Kh7 5 Kxh5 g3 6 Ra1 g2 7 Rg1 stops the pawn) 5 Ra5+ Ke4 6 Ra4+ Kd3 7 Ra3+ Kc2 8 Rg3! Rh7 9 Ra3, etc.

(b) If 1 Rh6? g3 wins on the spot.

(c) White fell for a fetching trap: 1 Kxh5? g3 2 Ra1 g2 3 Rg1 Kf6 4 Kh4 Kf5 5 Kh3 Kf4 6 Kh2 (if 6 Rxg2 Rh7 mate) Kf3 7 Rf1+ bxf1/B (underpromotion to avoid stalemate).

78. B is the correct answer.
Choices: (a) Kb7 (b) Kc7 (c) Ra2

(a) At first glance White appears to win easily by 1 Kb7 but this is foiled by the surprising defense 1...Re2! forcing White's rook away from its guard of f2. If 2 Rxe2 fxe2 3 a8/Q e1/Q 4 f4 Kg3=. Or 2 Rc5 Re8 3 a8/Q Rxa8 4 Kxa8 Kxf2=.

(b) White won with 1 Kc7! Re7+ (1...Re2 no longer works because of 2 Rxe2 fxe2 3 a8/Q WITH CHECK; or 1...Kf1 2 Kb7 Re2 3 Rc1+ followed by a8/Q) 2 Kb8 Re8+ 3 Rc8 Rxc8+ 4 Kxc8 Kxf2 5 a8/Q and Black's pawn is only on the sixth rank instead of the seventh (which would draw).

(c) White's task is hard after 1 Ra2 Kf1 because 2 a8/Q? Rxa8 3 Rxa8 Kxf2 always draws; and if 2 Kc6 Kg2.

79. A is the correct answer.
Choices: (a) b6 (b) Kb3 (c) Rf8+

(a) Since both alternatives lose quickly, White found the only draw by 1 b6! Ra6 (but not 1...g1/Q? 2 Rxg1 Kxg1 3 b7 and queens) 2 Rf8+ with constant checks.

(b) Horrible is 1 Kb3 Rf4! stopping checks from behind. Now 2 b6 g1/Q 3 Rxg1 Kxg1 4 b7 Rf8 5 Kc4 Rb8 picks up the loner.

(c) Shun useless checks! Suicidal is 1 Rf8+? Kg3! 2 Rg8+ Rg4 with coronation imminent.

80. A is the correct answer.
Choices: (a) Kc5 (b) Re1 (c) f4

(a) White won elegantly with 1 Kc5! h4 2 Rd1! h3 (no better is 2...Rxa7 3 Rd7+ Kb8 4 Kb6! Rxd7 5 cxd7 h2 6 d8/Q mate) 3 Rd7+ Kc8 4 Kb6 h2 5 Rxe7 Kd8 (to stop Re8 mate) 6 Rh7.

(b) White only loses time by 1 Re1? Kd8! (but not 1...Rxa7 2 Rxe7+ Kb6 3 Rxa7 Kxa7 4 Kd6! h4 5 c7 Kb7 6 Kd7) 2 Ra1 h4=.

(c) As usual, one tempo is crucial. Too slow is 1 f4? h4 2 Kc5 h3 3 Kb5 h2 4 Ka6 Rf8 5 Rh1 Rxf4 6 Rxh2 Ra4+ 7 Kb5 Rxa7=.

81. B is the correct answer.
Choices: (a) h7 (b) Rf3+ (c) Rh2

(a) Black gets a perpetual after the hasty 1 h7? Rg4+ 2 Kh5 Rg5+ 3 Kh6 Rg6+.

(b) White won by forcing a king and pawn ending: 1 Rf3+! Kg6 2 Rg3+ Rxg3 3 Kxg3 Kxh6 4 Kg4 Kg6 5 Kf4 Kg7 (or 5...f5 6 Ke5 Kg5 7 f3 Kg6 8 f4 followed by Kxf5) 6 Kf5 Kf7 7 f3 gaining the opposition.

(c) Alas 1 Rh2? Kg6! costs White his passed pawn.

82. A is the correct answer.
Choices: (a) e6+ (b) Kd5 (c) Kb6

(a) The path to glory is 1 e6+! Kxe6 2 Kc6 Ra8 3 d7 Ra6+ 4 Kb7 Kxd7 5 c8/Q+.

(c) Tempting but wrong is 1 Kd5? Ra8! 2 e6+ Kc8 3 Kc6 Ra6+=.

(c) Too slow is 1 Kb6? Rh8 2 Kb7 Re8 3 e6+ Kxe6 4 c8/Q+ Rxc8 5 Kxc8 Kxd6=.

83. B is the correct answer.
Choices: (a) Rd8 (b) Rb8 (c) Rh8

(a) On 1 Rd8? Ke1 2 Kc4 Ra6 3 Re8+ Kf2 forces an immediate draw.

(b) A gorgeous, complex win is achieved by 1 Rb8! Rd6+ 2 Kc3 Rc6+ 3 Kb2 Rc2+ (or 3...Ra6 4 a8/Q Rxa8 5 Rxa8 Ke2 6 Re8+ Kf2 7 Kc2 stops the pawn) 4 Kb3 Kc1 5 a8/Q Rb2+ 6 Ka3 d1/Q (the best chance; if 6...Rxb8 7 Qxb8 d1/Q 8 Qb2 mate!) 7 Qc6+! (a clever trap is 7 Rxb2? Qf3+! 8 Qxf3 stalemate!) Rc2 8 Qh6+ Rd2 (if 8...Qd2 9 Qh1+ Qd1 10 Rb1+ Kxb1 11 Qxd1+ wins) 9 Rc8+ Kb1 10 Qb6+ Ka1 11 Qf6+ Rd4 (or 11...Kb1 12 Rb8+) 12 Qxd4+! Qxd4 13 Rc1 mate!

(c) On 1 Rh8 Rd6+ 2 Kc4 Ra6 3 a8/Q Rxa8 4 Rxa8 Ke2 5 Ra2 Ke1 compels White to give up his rook for the pawn.

84. A is the correct answer.
Choices: (a) a5 (b) Kc8 (c) Rd8

(a) The two split pawns remind one of split pins in bowling. In this notorious ending White cannot force a win against best defense, but Black just erred by moving his king from a7 to a6 (see diagram 98 for a similar position where White has no a-pawn). Now 1 a5! Kxa5 (too late for Herpicide after 1...Ka7 2 Kd6+ Ka8 3 Rd8+ Ka7 4 c7) 2 Kb7 Rb1+ 3 Ka7 Rc1 4 c7 wins.

(b) The game was drawn after 1 Kc8? Kb6! 2 c7 Kc6 3 a5 Rh8+ 4 Rd8 Rh7 5 a6 Rxc7+ 6 Kb8 Rg7 7 Re8 (if 7 a7 Rb7+ 8 Ka8 Rb1 locks in the king) Kb6 8 Re6+ Kb5 9 a7 Rg8+=.

(c) On 1 Rd8? Ka7!= repairs the damage and saves the draw (but not 1...Rh7+? 2 Kb8 Kb6 3 c7 Rxc7 4 Rd6+ Rc6 5 a5+! Kb5 6 Rxc6 Kxc6 7 a6 wins).

85. C is the correct answer.
Choices: (a) Ra1 (b) Ra4+ (c) Rf2+

(a) Black cannot afford to let White improve the awkward position of his rook by 1...Ra1? 2 Re6.

(b) Horizontal checks merely afford the king shelter after 1...Ra4+? 2 Kg3 Ra3+ 3 Kg4 Ra4+ 4 Kh5 Rf4 5 Rg6+ Kf7 6 f6, etc.

(c) The temporary immobility of White's rook can be exploited by 1...Rf2+! 2 Ke3 Rg2 3 Rg6+ Kf7 4 Kf3 Rg1 5 Kf2 Rg4 (since the rook can't be dislodged, the king now heads for d5) 6 Kf3 Rg1 7 Kf4 Rf1+ 8 Ke5 Re1+ 9 Kd5 Rg1 10 Rf6+ Kg7 11 Ke6 Re1+! (avoiding 11...Rxg5? 12 Rf7+ Kh6 13 Rf8 Rg1 14 f6 Ra1 15 Rh8+ Kg6 16 Rg8+ followed by f7) 12 Kd6 (or 12 Kd7 Re5! 13 Kd6 Ra5) Rg1 13 Rg6+ Kf7 14 Kd7 Rg2

15 Rf6+ Kg7 16 Rd6 Rxg5 17 Ke6 Rg1 18 Ke7 (or 18 f6+ Kg6 19 Ke7 Rf1 20 Re6 Rf2 21 Re1 Ra2! 22 Rg1+ Kh7=) Rf1 19 Rg6+ Kh7=.

86. C is the correct answer.
Choices: (a) Kxa7 (b) Ka6 (c) Kc5

(a) On 1...Kxa7? Kc7 Black is helpless against the threat of Ra1+.

(b) If 1...Ka6? 2 Kc7! Rxa7+ 3 Kc6 the threat of mate by Ra1 is again fatal.

(c) Exact defense is required. The saving grace is 1...Kc5! 2 Rb7 Rh8! 3 Kc7 (if 3 Rb8 Rh7+ followed by Rxa7) Ra8! 4 Kd7 Rh8= with a seesaw balance.

87. A is the correct answer.
Choices: (a) Rd8 (b) Rb8+ (c) Rh8

(a) Black faces certain defeat unless his king gets to the queenside pronto: 1...Rd8! 2 Rc4 (2 Rxd8 Kxd8 3 Kc6 Kc8 4 a6 Kb8=) Rb8+! (but not 2...Kd7? 3 a6 Rc8 4 a7!) 3 Ka4 (or 3 Ka6 Kd7=) Kd7 4 a6 Rc8! 5 Rb4 Rh8! (but not 5...Kc7? 6 Rb7+ Kc6 7 Ka5) 6 Ka5 Kc7 7 a7 (if 7 Rb7+ Kc8! 8 Kb6 Rh6+ 9 Ka7 Rf6 holds White at bay) Rh5+ 8 Ka6 Rh6+ 9 Ka5 Rh5+=.

(b) Premature is 1...Rb8+? 2 Kc6 Rb1 3 a6 Ra14 Kb6 Rb1+ 5 Ka5! Ra1+ 6 Ra4 and wins.

(c) Inadequate is 1...Rh8? 2 a6 Rh1 3 Ka5 as in "b".

88. A is the correct answer.
Choices: (a) Ra1 (b) Rb1 (c) Re2

(a) This important theoretical ending has occurred many times. The rook must check on the seventh rank by staying as far away as possible: 1...Ra1! 2 Rd8 Ra7+ 3 Rd7 Ra8!

(otherwise 3...Ra6? 4 Ke8+ Kf6 5 e7 Ra1+ 6 Rd8 Ra7 7 Rd6+ wins) 4 Rb7 Kg6! 5 Kd7 Kf6! 6 Rc7 (or 6 e7 Kf7 7 Rc7 Re8 8 Kd6 Ra8!) Kg7! 7 Kd6+ Kf8 8 Rh7 Ra6+=.

(b) The danger of getting too close with the rook is illustrated by 1...Rb1? 2 Rd8 Rb7+ 3 Rd7 Rb8 4 Rd1 Rb7+ 5 Kd8 Kf6 6 e7! Rb8+ 7 Kd7 Rb7+ 8 Kd6 Rb6+ 9 Kc7 Re6 10 Kd8 Rxe7 11 Rf1+ Ke6 12 Re1+ Kd6 13 Rxe7 and wins.

(c) Black can't sit back and wait by 1...Re2? 2 Rd8 Re1 3 Kd7 Rd1+ 4 Ke8 Re1 5 e7, etc.

89. C is the correct answer.
Choices: (a) h3 (b) Kc7 (c) Rg3+

(a) Black resigned after 1...h3? 2 Rd3! Rxd3 3 f8/Q Rg3+ 4 Kh7 Kd5 5 Qf5+ Kc6 6 Qe6+ in view of 6...Kb7 7 Qd7+ Ka8 8 Qc8+ Ka7 9 Qc7+ picking up the rook.

(b) Another error is 1...Kc7? 2 Re2! Kd7 (if 2...h3 3 Kg7 Rg3+ 4 Kf6 Rf3+ 5 Ke7 wins) 3 Re8 followed by f8/Q.

(c) Now is the time to entomb the king in front of his own pawn by a series of timely checks with 1...Rg3+ 2 Kf6 Rf3+ 3 Kg7 Rg3+ 4 Kf8 h3! 5 Re2 Kd7=.

90. B is the correct answer.
Choices: (a) Kg4 (b) Ke4 (c) Ke5

(a) Black lost after 1...Kg4? 2 b7 f5 (or 2...Rb8 3 Kc7 Rxb7+ 4 Kxb7 f4 5 Kc6) 3 b8/Q Rxb8 4 Rxb8 f4 5 Kd5 f3 6 Ke4 f2 7 Rf8 Kg3 8 Ke3.

(b) The only good defense is 1...Ke4! 2 b7 f5 3 b8/Q Rxb8 4 Rxb8 f4 5 Rb4+ Ke3 6 Kd5 f3 7 Ra3+ Ke2 8 Ke4 f2 9 Ra2+ Ke1 10 Ke3 f1/N+! 11 Kd3 Ng3 with a book draw. (See diagram 151.)

(c) Black can't afford to lose a tempo with 1...Ke5? 2 b7 f5 3 b8/Q Rxb8 4 Rxb8 f4 5 Kc5 f4 6 Kc4 f3 7 Kd3 easily catching the pawn.

91. C is the correct answer.
Choices: (a) Rc8 (b) Rh8 (c) Kc6

(a) The game was drawn after 1...Rc8? 2 Rc7! Rf8+ 3 Kg6 Kd4 4 Kg7 Rb8 5 h8/Q Rxh8 6 Kxh8 d5 7 Kg7 Kd3 8 Kf6=.

(b) Some critics maintain that 1...Rh8 "wins easily." However 2 Rc7! Kd4 3 Kg6 d5 4 Kg7 Rd8 5 h8/Q Rxh8 6 Kxh8 Kd3 7 Kg7 d4 8 Kf6 Kd2 9 Ke5 d3 10 Kd4 c2 11 Rc3 Ke2 12 Ke4 holds the draw.

(c) The correct continuation is 1...Kc6! 2 Ra7 Rh8! 3 Ra3 Rxh7 4 Rxc3+ Kd5 5 Rd3+ Kc5 and White can't get his king back in time (if 6 Ke4 Re7+ 7 Kf4 d5).

92. A is the correct answer.
Choices: (a) Kb5 (b) Kb7 (c) Kc5

(a) Black is in dire straits, yet he drew this famous ending: 1...Kb5! 2 h3 (if 2 h4 Rb3+ 3 Kf4? Rb4+ 4 Kf5 Ra4! turns the tables) Kb4 3 Kf4 (Black just gets back in time on 4 Kh4 Kb3 5 g5 Rb1 6 Kh5 a1/Q 7 Rxa1 Rxa1 8 g6 Kc4 9 g7 Rg1 10 Kh7 Ke6 11 g8/Q+ Rxg8 12 Kxg8 Kf5=) Rc2! 4 Rb8+ Kc3 7 Ra8 Kb4 and a draw was agreed because White can't cope with the remarkable threat of Rc4+ followed by Ra4.

(b) Retreating costs a vital tempo: 1...Kb7? 2 Ra4 Kb6 3 h3 Kb5 4 Ra8 Kb4 5 Kh4 and Black is a move behind the line shown in "a".

(c) Black steps on his own toes by 1...Kc5? 2 h4 Kb4 3 Kf4 (this exit would not be possible with Black's king on b5 because of 3...Rb4+ followed by Ra4).

93. B is the correct answer.
Choices: (a) Rh7+ (b) Kg4 (c) Kh4

(a) It should be easy to eliminate 1...Rh7+? 2 Ke6 Rh8 3 Rc8.

(b) Black drew after 1...Kg4! 2 Kf6 (or 2 Rc8 Rh7+ 3 Ke6 Rxd7 4 Kxd7 Kf4! 5 Ke6 6 g4 6 Rc4+ Kf3 7 Kf5 g3 8 Rc3+ Kf2 9 Kf4 g2 10 Rc2+ Kf1 11 Kf3 g1/N+! with a book draw) Rf8+! (but not 2...Rh6+? 3 Ke5 Rh8 4 Rc8) 3 Ke6 Rd8 4 Rd5 Kf4 5 Rf5+ Kg4 6 Rf7 Kh3 7 Kf5 g4 8 Kf4 g3 9 Kf3 Kh4!=.

(c) A instructive trap is 1...Kh4? 2 Rc8 Rh7+ 3 Ke6 Rxd7 4 Kxd7 g4 5 Ke6 g3 6 Kf5 g2 7 Kf4 g1/Q 8 Rh8 mate.

94. A is the correct answer.
Choices: (a) Kf4 (b) Ke5 (c) Rh8+

(a) The surest way to draw is 1...Kf4! 2 Ra4+ Kf3! 3 Rb4 (not 3 g5? Rh8 mate!) Rh8+ 4 Kg5 Rg8+ 5 Kf5 Rf8+ 6 Ke5 Rg8, etc.

(b) Black lost after 1...Ke5? 2 Ra6! Kf4 3 Rf6+ Ke5 4 g5 Rh8+ 5 Kg4 followed by Rf1 and the advance of the pawn and king.

(c) A more difficult drawing line is 1...Rh8+ 2 Kg3 Ke5! (not 2...Rg8 3 Ra5!) 3 Rf3 (or 3 Ra6 Rb8) Ke6 4 g5 Ke7 5 Kg4 Rf8!

95. C is the correct answer.
Choices: (a) Rc3 (b) Ra2 (c) a2

(a) Black has three plausible ways to defend the pawn. Two lose! If 1...Rc3? 2 h5+ Kf6 3 Kh4 White slowly mobilizes his two passed pawns.

(b) In the game Black lost after 1...Ra2? 2 Kg4 Ra1 3 Ra6+ Kf7 4 Kg5 a2 5 g4 Ke7 6 Ra7+ Ke8 7 h5 Kf8 8 h6 Rb1 9 Rxa2.

(c) Chigorin later pointed out that it's necessary to tie White's rook to the a-file to achieve a difficult draw by 1...a2! 2 h5+ Kf6 3 Kh4 (if 3 g4 Rc5! 4 Rxa2 Kg5 leads to a theoretical draw) Rh2+ 4 Kg4 Rb2 5 Ra6+ Kf7 6 Kg5 Rb5+ 7 Kh4 Rb2 8 g4 Rc2 9 g5 (or 9 h6 Rc6!=) Rc4+ 10 Kg3 Rc3+ 11 Kf4 Rc4+ 12 Ke3 Rh4 13 h6 (or 13 g6+ Kg7 14 Ra7+ Kg8) Rg4=.

96. C is the correct answer.
Choices: (a) Rg7 (b) Kh7 (c) Ra6+

(a) Black went down without a fight after 1...Rg7? 2 Re8+ Kh7 3 Re7 Rxe7 4 Kxe7 Kh7 5 h5 Kg8 6 Kf6 Kh7 7 Kf7 Kh8 8 Kg6.

(b) No better is 1...Kh7? 2 Re7+ Rxe7 3 Kxe7 Kg6 4 Ke6.

(c) The only hope is 1...Ra6+! 2 Re6 Ra4 3 Kf5 Kg7 4 Re7+ Kf8 5 Rh7 Ra6. To make progress White will have to play g5 whereupon, after an exchange of pawns, Black reaches the book draw shown in diagram 52.

97. C is the correct answer.
Choices: (a) Kd3 (b) Kd1 (c) c3

(a) Black lost after 1...Kd3? 2 Kf2! Kd2 (too late now for 2...c3 3 Ke1! c2 4 Rh3+ Ke4 5 Kd2) 3 Rxh2 c3 4 Kf1+ Kd1 5 Rh8 c2 6 Rd8+ Kc1 7 Ke2 Kb2 8 Rb8+ and wins. Even masters go astray in these "simple" endings.

(b) A costly mistake that tosses away the draw is 1...Kd1? 2 Rxh2 c3 3 Ke3 c2 4 Rh1 mate.

(c) After 1...c3! 2 Rxh2+ Kb1! 3 Ke3 c2 White must sacrifice his rook for the pawn leading to an elementary draw.

98. A is the correct answer.
Choices: (a) Ra8 (b) Ra7+ (c) Ra5

(a) A move to remember is 1...Ra8! 2 Kf7 (or 2 f7 Kg7) Kh6 3 Re1 Ra7+ 4 Re7 Ra8! 5 Rd7 Kh7 6 Rd1 Ra7+ 7 Ke6 Ra6+ 8

Rd6 Ra8! 9 Rd4 Kg8 10 Rg4+ Kf8 and a draw was agreed. (Even if White has an extra h-pawn, this ending can still be drawn with best defense. See diagram 84.)

(b) Everything else loses! If 1...Ra7+? 2 Kf8 Kg6 3 f7+ Kh7 4 Re1 Ra8+ (or 4...Kg6 5 Kg8! Rxf7 6 Rg1+ Kf6 7 Rf1+ and Rxf7 snares the rook) 5 Ke7 Ra7+ 6 Kf6 Ra6+ 7 Re6 Ra8 8 Re8 Ra6+ 9 Ke5 and Black will run out of checks.

(c) Utterly futile is 1...Ra5? 2 f7 Ra7+ 3 Kf6 Ra8 4 Re8.

99. A is the correct answer.
Choices: (a) Ra6+ (b) h4 (c) Kg6

(a) In an apparently hopeless predicament Black garnered the brilliancy prize: 1...Ra3+! 2 Kg2 Kg4! 3 a7 Ra2+ 4 Kg1 Kf3 5 Kh1! (or 5 f5 Rg2+ 6 Kh1 Rg7! 7 f6 Rf7 8 Kh2 Kf4 9 Kh3 Kf5 10 Kh4 Kxf6 11 Kxh4 Kf5=) h4! 6 f5 Kg3! 7 Rg8+ Kh3! 8 a8/Q Ra1+! 9 Qxa1 stalemate!

(b) Too slow is 1...h4 2 a7 with the devastating threat of Rf8+ and Black's king has no place to hide.

(c) Retreating loses: 1...Kg6? 2 a7 Kh7 3 f5 h4 4 f6 h3 5 f7 h2 (or 5...Rf1+ 6 Kg3 Rxf7 7 Rh8+! Kxh8 8 a8/Q+ wins in the long run) 6 Rh8+! Kxh8 7 f8/Q+ Kh7 8 Qf7+ Kh6 9 Qf6+ Kh8 10 Qxa1.

100. A is the correct answer.
Choices: (a) Rh2 (b) Ra2 (c) Rb2

(a) The pawns can't be stopped, but constant mating threats prevent White from queening any of them! The only way to draw is 1...Rh2! 2 Kf1 (or 2 Kd1 Kd3 3 Kc1 Kc3 4 Kb1 Rb2+ 5 Ka1 Rb6! 6 a7 Ra6+ 7 Kb1 Rb6+ 8 Kc1 Rh6!) Kf3 3 Kg1 Rg2+ 4 Kh1 Rg8 5 a7 Rh8+ 6 Kg1 Rg8+ 7 Kf1 Rh8! 8 Ke1 Ke3 9 Kd1 Kd3 10 Kc1 Kc3 11 Kb1 Rh1+ 12 Ka2 Rh2+ 13 Ka3 Rh1 14 Ka4 Kc4 15 Ka5 Kc5 and White's king must turn back because if 16 Ka6? Ra1 mates.

(b) The wrong way is 1...Ra2? 2 Kd1 Kd3 3 Kc1 Kc3 4 b8/Q Ra1+ 5 Qb1!

(c) Also inadequate is 1...Rb2 2 Kd1 Kd3 3 Kc1 Kc3 4 a7 Rh2 (or 4...Ra2 5 b8/Q Ra1+ 6 Qb1 as in "b") 5 Kd1 Kd3 6 Ke1 Ke3 7 Kf1 Kf3 8 Kg1 Rg2+ 9 Kh1 and a pawn queens on the next turn.

101. A is the correct answer.
Choices: (a) 1 Qh1+ (b) Qd8+ (c) Qh5+

(a) Many rook and pawn endings resolve into queen vs. rook after a pawn is promoted. The winning method is not always easy: first the king and rook must be forced to an edge of the board; the rook must eventually separate itself and then the queen can pick it up by a series of timely checks.

Here all choices win, the most efficient is 1 Qh1+! Kg8 2 Qh5! (this quiet move compels the rook to skedaddle; too hasty is 2 Qh6 Rf7+ 2 Kg6? Rf6+! 3 Kxf6 stalemate!) Ra7 (there is no safe port; if 2...Rh7? 3 Qe8 mate; or 2...Rg1 3 Qd5+ Kh8 4 Qa8+ Kh7 5 Qa7+ Kh6 7 Qxg1) 3 Qd5+ Kh7 4 Qh1+ Kg8 5 Qg1+ followed by Qxa7.

(b) Closing in too soon prolongs the agony: 1 Qd8+ Kh7 2 Qf8 Rg6+ 3 Kf7? Rf6+! 4 Kxf6 stalemate.

(c) The win takes longer after 1 Qh5+ Kg8 2 Qh6?! Rf7+ 3 Kg6? (necessary is 3 Ke6 Re7+! 4 Kd6! to avoid stalemate) Rf6+! 4 Kxf6=.

102. C is the correct answer.
Choices: (a) Rf8 (b) Rh7 (c) Rg7

(a) Black's task is eased by 1 Rf8? Qg5+ 2 Kh7 Ke7 3 Rg8 Qxf5+.

(b) The pawn falls after 1 Rh7? Qg5+ 2 Rg7 Qxf5 and the rest is a matter of technique.

(c) Sometimes a rook and pawn can draw if the pawn can be held. White can build an impenetrable fortress to deny Black's king access to the seventh rank by 1 Rg7! Ke5 2 Rf7 Kf4 3 Rf8 Kg5 4 Rf7 Qd6 5 Kg7=.

103. C is the correct answer.
Choices: (a) Kd6 (b) Kf6 (c) Ke6

(a) Temping but untenable is 1 Kd6? Kf4! (but not 1...Kd4 2 Kd7 drawing as in "c") 2 Kd7 Qd2+ 3 Kc7 Qc3+ 4 Kd7 Qd4+ 5 Kc7 Qe5+ 6 Kd7 Qd5+ 7 Kc7 Qe6! 8 Kd8 Qd6+ 9 Ke8 (White is forced to block his own pawn) Kf5 and wins.

(b) The same zigzag maneuver occurs on 1 Kf6? Kd4! (but not 1...Kf4? 2 Kf7= and the pawn can't be stopped) 2 Kf7 Qf2+ 3 Kg7 Qg3+ 4 Kf7 Qf4+ 5 Kg7 Qe5+ 6 Kf7 Qf5+ 7 Kg7 Qe6! 8 Kf8 Qf6+ 9 Ke8 Ke5, etc.

(c) An incredible save is 1 Ke6! Kf4+ (or 1...Kd4+ 2 Kd7) 2 Kf7 and the awkward placement of Black's king blocks his queen from giving the necessary checks.

104. B is the correct answer.
Choices: (a) Qd3+ (b) Qb3 (c) Qg1+

(a) The trick is to force the king in front of the pawn and then close in for the kill with the king, gaining a tempo each time. Yet the zigzag maneuver doesn't work here in view of 1 Qd3+? Kc1! 2 Kf3 Kb2 3 Qb5+ Ka2 4 Qc4+ Kb2 5 Qb4+ Ka1 6 Qc3+ Kb1 7 Qb3+ Ka1! 8 Qxc2 stalemate!

(b) The right way is 1 Qb3! Kd2 2 Qb2 Kd1 3 Kf3! Kd2 (or 3...c1/Q 4 Qe2 mate) 4 Kf2 Kd1 5 Qd4+ Kc1 6 Qb4! Kd1 7 Qe1 mate. (Note that it would be drawn were White's king not so close to begin with.)

(c) The king can't be prevented from reaching a1 after 1 Qg1+? Kd2 (of course not 1...Ke2? 2 Qc1) 2 Qd4+ Kc1! 3 Kf3 Kb1 4 Qb4+ Ka1 5 Qc3+ Kb1 6 Qb3+ Ka1! 7 Qxc2 stalemate as in "a".

105. C is the correct answer.
Choices: (a) Qd3 (b) Qh1+ (c) Qh6

(a) With rare exceptions a queen can defeat a pawn that is two squares away from queening, but stalemate is always lurking. Not 1 Qd3? c2! 2 Qxc2=.

(b) White's badly placed king restricts the queen's mobility. Nothing is gained by 1 Qh1+? Kb2 2 Qb7+ Kc1! 3 Kf6 c2 4 Ke5 Kd1 5 Qd5+ Ke1! 6 Qa5+ Kd1 7 Qa4 Kd2 8 Qa2 Kc3!=.

(c) The right method is 1 Qh6! Kb2 (to prevent Qc1) 2 Qb6+ Kc1 3 Qe3+ Kb2 4 Qd4 Kb3 5 Kf6! c2 6 Qa1 and the king is now ready to close in for the kill.

106. A is the correct answer.
Choices: (a) Qa6 (b) Qf3 (c) Qd3+

(a) The queen usually defeats split pawns, but it requires a deft touch: 1 Qa6! Kc2 2 Qe2+ Kb3 (or 2...Kc3 3 Qf1 Kb3 4 Kc7 Ka2 5 Qxf2) 3 Qf3+! Kc2 (or 3...Kb4 4 Qd1) 4 Qxf2+ Kb3 and now comes the old zigzag maneuver — 5 Qe3+ Kc2 6 Qe2+ Kc1 7 Qc4+ Kd2 8 Qb3 Kc1 9 Qc3+ Kb1 10 Kc7 Ka7 11 Qc2 Ka1 12 Qa4+ Kb1 13 Kc6 and the king inches forward until the final reckoning. (Note that only a bishop or rook pawn on the seventh rank can draw if the White king is too far away.)

(b) A waste of time is 1 Qf3 Ka1 (threatening b1/Q) but White can still repair the damage by returning to 2 Qa3+ Kb1 3 Qa6! as in "a".

(c) White can go around in circles and check to his heart's content but eventually must bring his queen to a6 in order to win: 1 Qd3+ Ka2 2 Qa6+ Kb3 3 Qf1! as in "a".

107. B is the correct answer.
Choices: (a) Qxc5 (b) Qf4 (c) Qf3

(a) Black can draw after 1 Qxc5? c2 2 Kf7 Kb2 3 Qb4+ Ka1 4 Qc3+ Kb1 5 Qb3+ Ka1! 6 Qxc2 stalemate.

(b) Black's king can be forced to block the advance of his own pawn only by 1 Qf4! Kc2 (1...Kb2 2 Qe5! transposes to the main line) 2 Qe3! Kb2 3 Qe5! Kc2 (or 3...Kb3 4 Kf7 c2 5 Qa1) 4 Qxc5 and wins because the pawn can't reach the next rank (which would draw).

(c) Erroneous is 1 Qf3? Kb2 2 Qf6 Kc2! (not 2...Kb3 3 Qe5! c2 4 Qa1) 3 Qf2+ (or 3 Qe5 Kd2! 4 Qd5+ Kc1!) Kd1! 4 Qxc5 c2=.

108. B is the correct answer.
Choices: (a) Kb7 (b) Ka7 (c) Qe5+

(a) A bad mistake would be 1 Kb7? Kb2! 2 Ka6+ Kc2 3 Qe5 Kb1=.

(b) The right path is 1 Ka7! a3 2 Kb6 Kb2 3 Ka5+ Kc2 4 Qc7+ Kb2 5 Qb6+ Kc2 6 Qc5+ Kb2 7 Qb5+ Kc2 (if 7...Ka1 8 Kb4!) 8 Qxa3 Kb1 9 Qb3+ Ka1 10 Qd1+ Kb2 11 Kb4! a1/Q 12 Qd2+ Kb1 13 Kb3 and wins.

(c) After 1 Qb4? a3 2 Qxa3 Kb1 3 Qb3+ Ka1 Black either gets stalemated or queens his pawn.

109. A is the correct answer.
Choices: (a) Kd5 (b) Ke6 (c) a8/Q

(a) The king is a fighting piece — use it right! The only way to draw is 1 Kd5! Qc8 (if 1...Kb2 2 Kc6 Qa8+ 3 Kb6 Kb3 4 h8/Q! Qxh8 5 Kb7=) 2 Ke5 Qh8+ 3 Kd6! (but not 3 Kd5? Qxh7 4 a8/Q Qh1+ picking up the lady) Qa8 4 Ke6! (again not 4 Ke5? Qxa7 5 h8/Q Qa1+ and Qxh8) Qh8 5 Kd6 Kc2 6 Kc7 Qxh7+ 7 Kb8=.

(b) White cedes a decisive tempo with 1 Ke6? Kc2 2 Kd7 Kb3 3 Kc6 Kc4 4 Kb7 Qg7+ 5 Kb6 Qg6+ 6 Kb7 Qxh7+ 7 Kb8 Kb5! 8 a8/Q Kb6 and wins.

(c) White is a day late and a tempo short of getting his king to g7 after 1 a8/Q? Qxa8 2 Kf6 Qh8+ 3 Kg6 Kc2.

110. C is the correct answer.
Choices: (a) Qc4+ (b) Kc4 (c) Qc2

(a) White rejected 1 Qc4+ Ka3 2 Qc2? b1/Q 3 Qxb1 stalemate!

(b) The game was drawn after 1 Kc4? b1/Q 2 Qxb1+ Kxb1 3 Kb4 Kb2! (Yates overlooked this feint) 4 Kxa4 Kc3 5 f4 Kd4 6 f5 Ke5 catching the pawn.

(c) The right winning method is 1 Qc2! a3 (or 1...Ka3 2 Qb1 Kb3 3 f4 a3 4 f5 a2 5 Qd3+ Kb4 6 Qc3+ followed by Qxb2) 2 Kc3 Ka1 3 Kb3 b1/Q 4 Qxb1+ Kxb1 5 Kxa3 Kc2 6 f4 and this time the pawn can't be arrested.

111. A is the correct answer.
Choices: (a) Qg8 (b) Qe8 (c) Qf8

(a) Black is hoping for stalemate after 1 Qxa1? or 1 Qh2+? Ka8 fleeing from the mating net. A curious triangulation with the queen is the only way to win: 1 Qg8! Qa2! 2 Qe8! Qa4 3 Qe5+ Ka8 4 Qh8! threatening Ke7 mate. Now we have the diagram but with Black on move instead of White — see introduction. If 4...Qa1 5 Qxa1 WITH CHECK. Note that the journey of White's queen from h8-e8-e5-h8 forms a triangle.

(b) After 1 Qe8? Qg7! White, on move, can't extricate his king. Note that Black would lose if he were on move (2...Qh7 3 Qe5+ Ka8 4 Qa5+ Kb8 5 Qa7 mate).

(c) Also unsuccessful is 1 Qf8? Qa3! 2 Qe8 Qd6+ 3 Qd7 Qxd7+ 4 Kxd7=.

112. C is the correct answer.
Choices: (a) Kxb3+ (b) Qc4 (c) Qe2

(a) Although White is two pawns down, he should not be satisfied to draw with 1 Kxb3+? Kb1 2 Qa2+ Kc1=.

(b) Black also draws after 1 Qc4? Kb1 2 Qc3 Qf2 3 Qxb3+ Kc1.

(c) The trick is 1 Qe2! Qc2 (or 1...Qb1 2 Qe5+ b2 3 Qd5 c4 4 Qxc4) 2 Qe1+ Qb1 3 Qc3+ b2 4 Qc4! (zugzwang). If 4...Qd3+ (anything else is met by Qa2 mate) 5 Qxd3 b1/Q 6 Qc3 mates! A remarkable finale.

113. B is the correct answer.
Choices: (a) Qg6+ (b) Qg2+ (c) Qa8+

(a) Close but no cigar is 1 Qg6+? Kf8! (too obliging is 1...Qxg6+ 2 Kxg6 Kf8 3 Kf6 Ke8 4 Kxe6 Kd8 5 d7 Kc7 6 Ke7 forcing a new queen) 2 Qg5 Ke8=.

(b) Two well-timed checks and two quiet moves decide the issue: 1 Qg2+! Kf8 (or 1...Kh8 2 Qa8+ Qg8 3 Qxg8+ Kxg8 4 d7 puts the pawn out of reach) 2 Qa8+ Qe8 3 Qb7! Qd8 (or 3...Qf7 4 Qc8+! Qe8 5 d7) 4 Kg6! Qe8+ 5 Kf6 Qd8+ 6 Kxe6 Qe8+ 7 Qe7+ Qxe7 8 dxe7+ Ke8 9 Kd6 Kf7 10 Kd7 and the pawn queens.

(c) The lackluster 1 Qa8+ Qf8+ 2 Qxf8+ Kxf8 3 Kg6 Ke8 4 Kf6 Kd7 5 Ke5 Kd8! 6 Kxe6 Ke8 draws by holding the opposition, another reason why knowledge of king and pawn endings is essential.

114. A is the correct answer.
Choices: (a) Qb7 (b) Kxg3 (c) Kxh3

(a) Black promotes his pawn but cannot parry the mating threats after 1 Qb7! Kh2 (or 1...h2 2 Qe4! Kg1 3 Qe1 mate) 2 Qd7! g1/N (to stop Qxh3 mate) 3 Qd6! Ne2 4 Qd2 g2 5 Qxe2 Kh1 6 Qf3 h2 7 Qe4! Kg1 8 Qe1 mate.

(b) Black survives after 1 Kxg3? g1/Q+ 2 Kxh3 Qf1+=.

(c) Black is in fine shape after 1 Kxh3? g1/Q 2 Qb7+ g2 (if 3 Qc7? Qe3+)

115. B is the correct answer.
Choices: (a) Qh8+ (b) Qd5+ (c) Qe8+

(a) White runs out of checks and then is powerless to stop the enemy pawn from queening after 1 Qh8+? Kg4.

(b) White is clearly in danger because the b-pawn is so far advanced. Centralizing the queen is logical to ensure perpetual check, but there is another bonus: 1 Qd5+! Kh4 2 Qh1+ Kg4 3 Qg2+ Kh4 (or 3...Kf4 4 Qg3+ Ke4 5 Qg6+ and Qxc2) 4 Qh2+ Kg5 (or 4...Kg4 5 f3+! Kxf3 6 Qxc2) 5 f4+! and Black loses his queen!

(c) White only gets in trouble after 1 Qe8+? Kh4 2 Qd8+ Kg4 3 Qd4+ Kf3 4 Qe3+ Kg2 5 Qg3+ Kf1 6 Qh3+ Ke1.

116. C is the correct answer.
Choices: (a) Qxg5+ (b) Qg7+ (c) Qe6+

(a) White can't do better than draw after 1 Qxg5+? Kxg5 2 h3 Kf4 3 Kg7 Kf3 4 Kg6 Kxf2 5 Kf5 Kg3 6 Ke4 Kxh3 7 Kf3 Kh2 8 Kf2 h3 9 Kf1 etc.

(b) Trying to gain a tempo by 1 Qg7+ Kf5 2 h3 fails owing to Qxg7+ 3 Kxg7 Kg5! 4 Kf7 Kf5 holding the opposition.

(c) Since swapping queens doesn't win, White must find another path: 1 Qe6+! Kh5 (White gains the opposition after 1...Qf6+ 2 Qxf6+ Kxf6 3 h3! Kg5 4 Kg7 Kf4 5 Kg6 Kf3 6 Kg5 Kxf2 7 Kxh4 Ke3 8 Kg5) 2 Kh7! (a deadly quiet move) Qg2 3 Qf5+ Qg5 4 Qf3+ Qg4 5 Qf7+ Kg5 6 f4+! Qxf4 7 Qg6 mate!

117. A is the correct answer.
Choices: (a) Qb1 (b) Qf3 (c) Qc1+

(a) Two quiet moves capped by the gift of a pawn do the

trick: 1 Qb1! Kd4 (to stop Qb5-d5 mate; if 1...Qf7 2 Qa2+ and Qxf7 wins) 2 Qb3! Qxe4+ 3 Kd6 Qa8 (if 3...Qg2 4 Qc3+ Ke4 5 Qc6+ nabs the queen) 4 Qe3+ Kc4 5 Qc3+ Kb5 6 Qb3+ Ka6 7 Qa4+ Kb7 8 Qb5+ Ka7 9 Kc7 wins.

(b) White only draws after1 Qf3? Kb4 2 Qc3+ Ka4.

(c) White has no more than perpetual check after 1 Qc1+? Kd3 2 Qc3+ Ke2 3 Qe3+ Kd1 4 Qf3+ Kxd2 5 Qf2+ Kd3 6 Qf3+ Kd4 7 Qf2+ Kd3 (not 7...Kxe4? 8 Qc2+ and Qxh7) etc.

118. B is the correct answer.
Choices: (a) Qe8 (b) Qc3 (c) f7

(a) Clearly 1 Qe8? Qg8+ 2 Ke7 Qxe8+ 3 Kxe8 g1/Q wins without a fuss.

(b) The only salvation is perpetual check when Black queens his pawn: 1 Qc3! Qg8+ 2 Ke7 g1/Q 3 f7+ Qg1g7 4 Qxh3+ Qg8h7 5 Qc8+ Qg7g8 6 Qc3+=.

(c) Shun 1 f7? Qa3+ 2 Ke8 Qe3+ 3 Kd7 Kg7 4 f8/Q+ Kxf8 5 Qf6+ Kg8 6 Qg6+ Kh8 7 Qf6+ Kh7 wriggling out.

119. B is the correct answer.
Choices: (a) Qh8 (b) a8/Q (c) Qf6+

(a) The actual game was drawn after 1 Qh8? Qd6+ 2 Kg4 Qe6+.

(b) White missed a surprising coup by 1 a8/Q! Qxa8 2 Qf6+ Kh7 3 g6+ Kh6 4 g7+ Kh7 (or 4...Kh5 5 Qf7+ Kh6 6 g8/N+!) 5 Qf8! Qd5 6 Qh8+ Kg6 7 g8/Q+.

(c) Even though White queens first he can't win after 1 Qf6+ Qxf6 2 gxf6 c2 3 a8/Q c8/Q=.

120. C is the correct answer.
Choices: (a) Qa2+ (b) Qc6+ (c) Qd5+

(a) White has no more than a draw after 1 Qa2+? Kb4 2 Qa3+ Kc4 3 Qa2+ etc.

(b) White gets nowhere fast with 1 Qc6+? Kb4.

(c) Black's king unexpectedly gets caught in a mating net after 1 Qd5+! Kb4 2 Qd3! Qc1 (zugzwang; if 2...Qa1 3 Qc3+ Ka4 4 b3+ and Qxa1 wins) 3 Qa3+ Kc4 4 b3+ Kd3 5 Qxc1.

121. B is the correct answer.
Choices: (a) Kh6 (b) Kg6 (c) Qxf5

(a) It's only a draw after 1 Kh6? Qc6 2 Qxc6 dxc6 3 Kxh5 Kf7 4 a4 Ke6 5 a5 Kd7 6 Kg5.

(b) A curious stair-movement enables White to win even though Black queens first: 1 Kg6! Qc6 2 Qxc6 dxc6 3 a4 f4 4 a5 f3 5 a6 f2 6 a7 f1/Q 7 a8/Q+ Qf8 8 Qa2+! Kh8 9 Qb2+ Kg8 10 Qc3+ Kg8 11 Qc4+ Kh8 12 Qd4+ Kg8 13 Qd7! and Black is in zugzwang!

(c) In a real game White, two pawns down, might well be tempted to snatch the draw by 1 Qxf5? Qxf5+ 2 Kxf5 h4 3 Kg4 Kf7 4 a4 Ke7 5 Kxh4.

122. B is the correct answer.
Choices: (a) Qe5+ (b) f3 (c) Qf7+

(a) White has nothing more than perpetual check after 1 Qe5+? Kg6 2 Qe4+ Kf7 3 Qh7+ Ke8 4 Qg8+ Kd7.

(b) The hapless position of Black's king paves the way for 1 f3! Qg6 (if 1...gxf3+ 2 Kh3! Qg6 3 g4+ Kg5 4 Qe5+ mates) 2 Qe5+ Qg5 3 Qe8+ Qg6 4 fxg4+ Kg5 5 Qe5+ Kxg4 6 Qf4+ Kh5 7 Qh4 mate.

(c) White has no more than a draw after 1 Qf7+? Qg6 2 Qe7 Qf5 3 Qe8+ Qg6.

123. C is the correct answer.
Choices: (a) Ka4 (b) Kb4 (c) Qc4+

(a) White can't stop the pawn from queening after 1 Ka4? Ka1.

(b) No better is 1 Kb4? Ka1 2 Qa6+ Qa2 3 Qf1+ b1/Q+.

(c) The only defense involves perpetual check or an amazing stalemate in the center of the board: 1 Qc4+! Ka1 2 Qa4+ Qa2 3 Kc5! b1/Q (if 3...Qxa4=) 4 Qd4+ Qbb2 5 Qd1+ Qab1 6 Qa4+=.

124. C is the correct answer.
Choices: (a) Qd5+ (b) Qb1+ (c) Qa6+

(a) White can't win after 1 Qd5+? Kc2! (for 1...Ke3? 2 Qe6+ see "c") 2 Qc4+ Kd1 3 Qb3+ Kc1 4 Qc3+ Kd1 5 Qa1+ Kc2=.

(b) Careless checks throw away the win: 1 Qb1+? Kc3 2 Qa1+ Kb3 3 Qb1+ and White must take the perpetual check.

(c) The queen is powerful enough to stop two advanced pawns: 1 Qa6+! Ke3 (forced; if 1...Kc2 2 Qxe2 wins) 2 Qe6+ Kf3 (or 2...Kd3 3 Qf5+ Kd4 4 Qf4+ Kd3 5 Qf3+ Kc2 6 Qxe2) 3 Qf5+ Ke3 4 Qf2+ Kd3 5 Qf3+ Kc2 6 Qxe2 Kc1 7 Qc4+ Kb2 8 Qd3 Kc1 9 Qc3+ Kd1 10 Kg2! Ke2 11 Qf3+ Ke1 12 Qf1 mate.

125. B is the correct answer.
Choices: (a) Qb8+ (b) Kg5 (c) Kg3

(a) Black unsnarls his queen from its passive post and wins after 1 Qb8+? Kh7 2 Qb2 Qf8.

(b) Transposing the move order secures a draw by 1 Kg5! Qh3 2 Qb8+ Kh7 3 Qh2! Qxh2 stalemate.

(c) Too slow is 1 Kg3? Kh7 followed by Kg6 and Black's

material superiority soon asserts itself.

126. A is the correct answer.
Choices: (a) Qh1 (b) Kb6 (c) Qh6

(a) The cornered king allows an ingenious "stair-stepper" combo: 1 Qh1! Qc8+ (or 1...Ka7 2 Qg1+ Ka8 3 Qg2! Ka7 4 Qg7+ and mates) 2 Kb6+ Kb8 3 Qh2+ Ka8 4 Qg2+ Kb8 5 Qg3+ Ka8 6 Qf3+ Kb8 7 Qf4+ Ka8 8 Qe4+ Kb8 9 Qe7! and Black is powerless against the immediate threat of Qa7.

(b) After 1 Kb6? Qe6+ 2 Kxa5 Kb7= the danger is over.

(c) The mating net vanishes after 1 Qh6? Qc8+ 2 Kb6 Qb8+ 3 Ka6 Qc8+=.

127. C is the correct answer.
Choices: (a) Kg3 (b) h5 (c) Qb5

(a) Material is even but Black's advantage lies in the fact that his b-pawn is more advanced than the a-pawn. After 1 Kg3? b3 2 Qb5 b2 3 Qb3 Kg7! 4 f4 (or 4 Qc2 Qe5+ 5 f4 Qe1+) Qd2 White must lose his queen.

(b) Unpalatable is 1 h5 gxh5 2 Qxh5 Qxf2.

(c) Some books maintain that White is lost. Yet if he can swap both queenside pawns — even at the cost of his h-pawn — then a draw is imminent because the remaining pawns are all on the same side of the board. Thus the best defense is 1 Qb5! Qxh4+ 2 Kg1 Qe4 3 a5 Qb1+ 4 Kh2 b3 5 a6 Qc2 6 Qd5 Qc7+ 7 g3 b2 8 Qb3 Qa7 9 Qxb2 Qxa6. Black is a pawn ahead but 3 vs. 2 is normally drawn with queens still on the board.

128. A is the correct answer.
Choices: (a) Qe3+ (b) Qb4+ (c) Qb1+

(a) A basic rule is that one side must be at least a rook ahead to force a win when there are no pawns left. Normally a queen and minor piece only draw against a lone queen, but this is a tactical exception: 1 Qe3+! Kf5 (or 1...Kd5 2 Qb3+ x-rays the queen) 2 Qf3+ Ke6 3 Qb3+ Ke7 4 Bg5+ Kf8 (on 4...Ke8 5 Qb8+ Kd7 6 Qb7+ wins) 5 Qb8+ Qe8 6 Qd6+ Kg8 7 Be7! and Black gets mated (7...Qf7 8 Qd8+).

(b) The king runs away to fight another day after 1 Qb4+ Kf3.

(c) The king is too elusive after 1 Qb1+? Ke5 2 Bc3+ Ke6 3 Qb3+ Ke7 4 Qb7+ (White no longer has Bg5+ as in "a") Ke6, etc.

129. C is the correct answer.
Choices: (a) Qh8+ (b) Be4 (c) Bd5

(a) Stalemate looms after 1 Qh8+ Qh7 2 Qd8 Qg8+! 3 Qxg8.

(b) The same goes for 1 Be4? Qh3+! 2 Kxh3.

(c) A quiet move does the trick: 1 Bd5! Qd1+ (or 1...Qg6+ 2 Kh4 and Black is in zugzwang) 2 Kh4 Qa4+ 3 Be4. Black either gets mated or drops his queen.

130. C is the correct answer.
Choices: (a) Qd5+ (b) Bd5+ (c) Bh7+

(a) Victory with queen and bishop against queen is possible only in exceptional circumstances. On 1 Qd5+? Kf4 Black can interpose his queen on any check because a bishop cannot beat a lone king once the queens are swapped.

(b) Another try that fails is 1 Bd5+? Kd4 2 Qc4+ Ke3 3 Qc3+ Kf4 4 Qf6+ Ke3 5 Kg3 Qb8+.

(c) The unfortunate constellation of king and queen lined up on the e-file allows a pretty win by 1 Bh7+! Kd4 (if 1...Kf4 2 Qg3 mate; or 1...Ke5 2 Qe3+ and Qxe8) 2 Qb4+ Kd5 3 Bg8+! Qxg8 (if 3...Kc6 4 Qa4+ or 3...Ke5 4 Qe1+ picks up the queen)

4 Qb3+ followed by Qxg8!

131. C is the correct answer.
Choices: (a) Kh5 (b) Qf6+ (c) Qe5+

(a) The task is easier when a king is cornered but approaching too fast allows stalemate with 1 Kh5? Qf7+! 2 Qxf7=.

(b) Black has a respite after 1 Qf6+ Qg7 2 Qd8+ Qg8 3 Qd6 Kg8.

(c) First comes a forcing series of checks, then the king invades: 1 Qe5+! Qg7 2 Qe8+ Qg8 3 Qh5+ Kg7 4 Qg6+ Kf8 5 Qd6+ Kg7 6 Kg5! Kh8+ (the best try) 7 Bg6 Qg7 8 Qb8+ Qg8 9 Qh2+ Kg7 10 Qh6 mate.

132. B is the correct answer.
Choices: (a) Be6+ (b) Qd5+ (c) Qd3+

(a) 1 Be6+ Kg6 2 Bf7+ Kf5 merely repeats the position.

(b) If Black could be forced to play g6, then Bf7+ would now win. This can be forced by 1 Qd5+! Kf4 (if 1...Kg4 2 Qf3+ Kh4 3 Qh1+ Kg4 4 Be6+ Kf4 5 Qc1+ snares the queen) 2 Qd4+ Kf5 3 Kf3! g6 (depriving the king an essential retreat but Black is in zugzwang; if 3...Qh6 4 Qd5+ Kf6 5 Qe6+ Kg5 6 Qe5+ Kh4 7 Qg3 mate) 4 Qd5+ Kf6 5 Qd8+ Kf5 12 Be6+ wins the queen. (Note: this is the initial position with the pawn on g6 instead of g7.)

(c) 1 Qd3+ Kf6 2 Qd8+ (nothing else still wins) Kg6 just repeats the position.

133. B is the correct answer.
Choices: (a) Qb6+ (b) Qb5+ (c) Qf8+

(a) The king skips out after 1 Qb6+? Kc8 2 Qb7+ Kd8 3 Bb6+ Ke8.

(b) Black has no time to breathe after 1 Qb5+! Kc8 2 Qe8+ Kc7 3 Bb6+ Kd6 4 Qf8+ Kc6 5 Qa8+ Kd6 6 Qd5+ Ke7 7 Bc5+ Ke8 8 Qg8+ Kd7 9 Kb7! and wins.

(c) Rule out 1 Qf8+? Qc8+ with a draw after queens are swapped.

134. B is the correct answer.
Choices: (a) Qf6+ (b) d7 (c) Qxg4+

(a) White can only repeat the position after 1 Qf6+ Kd5! (but not 1...Kd7 2 Qe7+ Kc6 3 Qe4+ followed by Qxa8) 2 Qd4+ Ke6.

(b) Sacrificing the pawn takes d7 away from the king after 1 d7! Bxd7 2 Qxg4+ Ke7 (2...Kd6 3 Qf4+ Kc5 4 Qb4+ leads to a similar demise) 3 Qxh4+ Kd6 4 Qf4+ Kc5 5 Qb4+ Kd5 6 Qd4+ Ke6 7 Qf6+ Kd5 8 Qf3+ followed by Qxa8.

(c) White has no more than a draw after 1 Qxg4+? Kxd6 2 Qf4+ Kd7.

135. A is the correct answer.
Choices: (a) c6+ (b) Qd6+ (c) h7

(a) White must sacrifice a pawn to deflect the king from guarding e6: 1 c6+! Kxc6 2 h7 a1/Q (to deflect the queen from e6) 3 Qxa1 Be6+ 4 Kb4! Qxh7 (if 4...Qd2+ 5 Qc3+ Qxc3 6 Kxc3 with h8/Q coming next) 5 Qa6+ Kd5 6 Qc4+ Ke5 7 Qc3+ Kd5 8 Qc5+ Kd7 9 Qa7+ followed by Qxh7!

(b) White has no more than a draw after 1 Qd6+ Ke8 2 Qe5+ Kf7.

(c) The reason for deflecting the king becomes clear in view of 1 h7? Be6+ followed by Qxh7.

136. C is the correct answer.
Choices: (a) e4 (b) Qg8+ (c) Bg2+

(a) Pointless is 1 e4? Qe5 (of course not 1...Qxe4? 2 Bg2) with an easy draw.

(b) Equally inconsequential is 1 Qg8+ Ka7 2 Bg2 Bd5.

(c) The quietus is 1 Bg2+! Bd5 (if 1...Ka7? 2 e4+ snares the queen; or 1...Kb8 2 Qh2+ Kc8 3 Bh3) 2 e4! Bxe4 3 Qb1! with a deadly cross-pin that nets a piece. White can win because his bishop is the "right color" to control a8.

137. A is the correct answer.
Choices: (a) Qc5 (b) Qb6+ (b) Bf5+

(a) Incredibly, only a quiet move works. Thus 1 Qc5! Qd1 (the best defense to the threat of Bc4+) 2 Bf5+ (but 2 Qc6+? Ke7! saves Black) Kf7 3 Bg6+ Ke6 4 Qc8+! Ke7 5 Qe8+ Kd6 6 Qd8+ x-rays the queen.

(b) No check can force a win! 1 Qb6+? Kd5! 2 Qd8+ Kc5 hangs on for dear life.

(c) The king reaches a safe port after 1 Bf5+? Kd5.

138. B is the correct answer.
Choices: (a) Nxc1 (b) Ng3+ (c) Qe6+

(a) No forced win after 1 Nxc1? Qb4+ for the simple reason that a queen and minor piece are insufficient against best defense.

(b) White bags the queen by 1 Ng3+! Ke5 2 Qf5+ Kd4 3 Qd7+ Kc3 (or 3...Ke3 4 Nf1+) 4 Ne4+.

(c) Black is off the hook after 1 Qe6+? Kf3 2 Nxc1 Qb4+.

139. B is the correct answer.
Choices: (a) Qe3+ (b) Nc6+ (c) Nd3+

(a) The king runs away and lives to fight another day after

1 Qe3+ Kf6 because queen and knight vs. queen is a book draw with best play.

(b) The unfortunate array of Black's forces leads to his downfall after 1 Nc6+ Kf5 (1...Kf6 2 Nd8+ costs his queen) 2 Qf2+ Ke4 (the best chance; if 2...Kg6 3 Ne5+ or 2...Ke6 3 Nd8+) 3 Qe3+ (but not 3 Qxf7? stalemate) Kd5 4 Qb3+ Ke4 5 Qd3+ Kf4 6 Qe3+ Kf5 7 Qf3+ Ke6 (or 7...Kg6 8 Ne5+) 8 Nd8+ with a family fork that finally nets the queen.

(c) No forced win is apparent after 1 Nd3+ Kf5 2 Qf2+ Ke6 3 Nc5+ Ke7. Eventually White will run out of checks or be forced to swap queens, whereupon a lone knight cannot force mate.

140. A is the correct answer.
Choices: (a) Qg6+ (b) Qc6+ (c) Qa4+

(a) White must act fast because the pawn is about to queen with mate no less. Yet the miracle of 1 Qg6+! Kd7 2 Qd3+! Qxd3 3 Nc5+ Kd6 4 Nxd3 remains a piece ahead and defuses the threat.

(b) It's only a draw after 1 Qc6+? Kf7 2 Nd8+ Kf8 (not 2...Qxd8 3 Qxc2) 3 Ne6+.

(c) The same goes for 1 Qa4+ Kf7 2 Nd8+ Kf8 3 Ne6+.

141. C is the correct answer.
Choices: (a) Qf3+ (b) Ne5+ (c) Ne3+

(a) White has no effective follow-up and remains two pawns down after 1 Qf3+? Kh4.

(b) White has nothing more than a draw by perpetual check after 1 Ne5+ Kg2 2 Qf3+ Kg1.

(c) Black's king is lured to the other side of the board where a decoy sacrifice seals his fate: 1 Ne3+! Kg3 2 Qg4+ Kf2 3 Qf4+ Ke2 4 Qf1+ Kd2 (of course not 4...Kxe3 5 Qe1+ followed by Qxe7) 5 Qd1+ Kc3 6 Qc2+ Kb4 7 Qb2+! Nb3 (if 7...Ka5 8 Nc4+ Ka6 9 Qb6 mate) 8 Qa3+!! Kxa3 9 Nc2 mate!

142. C is the correct answer.
Choices: (a) Nc6+ (b) Nf5+ (c) Ne6+

(a) White wins a piece but not the game after 1 Nc6+? Ke4 (forced; if 1...Ke6 2 Qg4+ skewers the queen) 2 Qd4+ Kf3 3 Nxa7 (more checks lead nowhere) Qc5+ =.

(b) A dead end is reached after 1 Nf5+? Ke5 when White would be wise to go for a draw by 2 Qd5+ Kxd5 3 Ne7+ and Nxc8.

(c) The right discovered check is hard to find: 1 Ne6+! Ke5 2 Qd4+ Kf5 (the knight always is immune in view of 2...Kxe6? 3 Qg4+ and Qxc8) 3 Qf4+ Kg6 4 Qg5+ Kf7 5 Qg7+ Ke8 6 Nc7+ Kd8 9 Kc6! (a lethal quiet move) Qf5 10 Qg8+ Ke7 11 Nd5+ wins.

143. A is the correct answer.
Choices: (a) Qf6 (b) Qg6+ (c) Qe6

(a) Although the pawn is doomed, Black's king is forced into a mating net after 1 Qf6! Qxe7 2 Qh8+ Qf8 3 Qh5+ Kd8 4 Qd1+ Kc7 5 Qc1+! (only so — but not 5 Qc2+? Kd6) Kb7 (or 4...Kd8 6 Qd2+ Kc7 7 Qa5+ Kb7 8 Qb5+ Ka7 9 Nc6+ Ka8 10 Qa6 mate) 6 Qc6+ Ka7 7 Qa4+ Kb7 8 Qb5+ and wins.

(b) No knockout punch is apparent after 1 Qg6+ Kxe7 2 Qg7+ Kd6! (but not 2...Kd8? 3 Qf8 mate).

(c) Tempting but good for no more than a draw is 1 Qe6? Qxe7 2 Qg8+ Qf8 3 Qg6+ Kd8. White can snag the knight but has no forced win.

144. B is the correct answer.
Choices: (a) Qxc7 (b) Qf3 (c) Qf4+

(a) Don't get sidetracked by going for the knight 1 Qxc7? Qf6=.

(b) The killer is 1 Qf3! Kg7 (if 2...Qa8 3 Qg4 threatening Nf5+ wins; or 1...Qg8 2 Nf5+ Kg5 3 Qg3+ snags the queen) 2 Qg4+ Kf8 3 Qc8+ Kg7 4 Nf5+ and Qxh8.

(c) Black escapes after 1 Qf4+? Kh5 2 Nf7 Qg7.

145. A is the correct answer.
Choices: (a) Qh7+ (b) Qd3+ (c) Qb3+

(a) White brutally demolishes the bishop and pawn before going after bigger game: 1 Qh7+! Kb2 (1...Kc3 2 Qg7+ d4 3 Qc7+ Kb2 4 Qb6+ transposes into the main line) 2 Qh8+ Ka2 3 Qxa8+ Kb2 4 Qb7+ Kc2 5 Qh7+ Kb2 6 Qg7+ Ka2 7 Qa7+ Kb2 8 Qd4+ Ka2 9 Qxd5+ Kb2 10 Qb3+ Kc1 11 Qd1+ Kb2 12 Nc4+ (the pawn is no longer on d5!) Ka2 13 Qc2+ Qb2 14 Qxb2 mate.

(b) Remarkably, bringing the queen too close too soon only draws after 1 Qd3+? Kb2 2 Qb3+ Kc1 3 Qd1+ Kb2.

(c) Near and yet so far is 1 Qb3+? Kc1=.

146. A is the correct answer.
Choices: (a) Kg8 (b) Kg7 (c) Kh6

(a) There is only one way to profit from Black's lack of mobility: 1 Kg8! Qa7 2 Bd4! Qb8 (if 2...Qxd4 3 b8/Q+ Kxe7 4 Qxc7+ Kf6 5 Qxf7+ wins) 3 Bc5! f5 4 Kg7 f4 5 Kf6 f3 6 Bf2! (not 2 Be3? f2! 3 Bxf2 Qa7 4 Bxa7 stalemate) Qa7 (only move) 7 Bxa7 f2 8 b8/Q mate!

(b) Careless is 1 Kg7? Qa7 2 Kh8 (too late for 2 Bd4? Qxd4 WITH CHECK) Qb6 letting the queen out.

(c) White has no more than a draw after 1 Kh6? Qa7 2 Bd4 Qxd4! (not 2...Qb8? 3 Bc5! transposing into "a") 3 b8/Q+

Kxe7 4 Qxc7+ Kf6 5 Kh5=.

147. A is the correct answer.
Choices: (a) Bf4+ (b) Be3 (c) Nc6+

(a) A queen can beat two minor pieces most of the time, but here the most powerful piece on the board is helpless because she lacks mobility: 1 Bf4+! Ka7 2 Be3+ Kb8 3 Kd8! and Black is in zugzwang (3...Qa7 4 Nc6+ Ka8 5 Nxa7).

(b) It's only a draw after 1 Be3? Qa7+! 2 Bxa7+ Kxa7 3 Kc6 e3 4 Kb5 e2 5 Nd3 Ka8 and the king can't be dislodged because the knight is tied down.

(c) Another draw results from 1 Nc6+? Qxc6+ 2 Kxc6 Ka7 3 Kb5 e3 4 Bxe3+ Ka8. White's bishop is the "wrong color" to control a8.

148. B is the correct answer.
Choices: (a) b7 (b) a8/Q (c) Kxh2

(a) White gets mated unceremoniously after 1 b7? Qxe1+ 2 Kxh2 Kf3 3 b8/Q Qf2+ 4 Kh3 Qg2+ 4 Kh4 Qg4.

(b) Stalemate again rears its ugly head after 1 a8/Q! Qxa8 2 b7 Qa7 (or 2...Qxd8 3 b8/Q+! Qxb8 4 Bg3+ Kxg3=) 3 Bf2! Qb8 4 Bg3+! Kxg3 5 Nc6 Qxb7 stalemate! (White has no legal move and is NOT in check.)

(c) Plausible but wrong is 1 Kxh2? Kf3! 2 Kh3 (or 2 Bd2 Qe5+) Qa4! 3 a8/Q+ (the only way to stave off an immediate mate) Qxa8 4 Ne6 Qc8 and wins.

149. C is the correct answer.
Choices: (a) g3+ (b) Bf2+ (c) Bf6+

(a) White loosens his position disastrously after 1 g3+? Kg5.

(b) Black's king escapes on 1 Bf2+? Kg5. Soon the queen

will hold sway.

(c) The beauty lies in the repeated zugzwangs that precede mate: 1 Bf6+! g5 2 Kh2! Qxe2 3 Bc3! (the first zugzwang) Qf2 4 Be5! (the second threatens Bg3 mate) Qe1 (or 4...g4 5 Bf6 mate) 4 g3+ Qxg3+ 5 Bxg3 mate.

150. A is the correct answer.
Choices: (a) a7+ (b) Bf3 (c) Kg3

(a) Ordinarily two minor pieces are no match for a queen but the saving resource is 1 a7+! Kxb7 2 a8/Q+! Kxa8 3 Nb6+! cxb6 4 Bf3 Qxf3 stalemate!

(b) Transposing moves is costly: 1 Bf3? Qxf3 2 a7+ Kxb7 3 a8/Q+ Kxa8 4 Nb6+ Kb7 and White cannot get rid of his knight to claim stalemate.

(c) Trying for more than a draw loses after 1 Kg3? Qd3+ 2 Bf3 Qxa6.

151. A is the correct answer.
Choices: (a) Ng6+ (b) Nf7+ (c) Kh7

(a) After the smoke clears, Rook and pawn endings often convert to rook vs. knight without pawns on the board. This is usually drawn even in a worst case scenario with a king on the edge of the board: 1 Ng6+! Kf6 2 Nh4! (but 2 Nf4? Rh1+ 3 Nh5+ Kf5 costs the pinned knight because White is in zugzwang) Rh1 3 Kh5 Rg1 4 Nf3 Rg3 5 Nh4 Rg5+ 6 Kh6=.

(b) Rule out 1 Nf7+? Kf6 2 Nd6 Rh1 mate.

(c) Rule out 1 Kh7 Kf6 suffocating the knight (2 Kh6 Rh1 mate).

152. A is the correct answer.
Choices: (a) Bb8 (b) Bd6 (c) Kxe2

(a) Rook vs. bishop is usually drawn provided the king heads for a corner which is OPPOSITE the color of its bishop. A rook plus a pawn wins if the pawn has not advanced too far. Here White must prevent the rook from getting BEHIND its pawn (on the f-file) while the bishop stands ready to give check if and when the Black king goes to g3.

The only correct square is 1 Bb8! Re8 (if 1...Rb2 2 Bd6! Rc2 3 Be5 Rd2 4 Bf4 Re2 leads again to the diagram) 2 Bg3! (but not 2 Ba7? Kg3! — see "b") Kg4 (if 2...Kxg3 is stalemate — the saving resource!) 3 Kxf2 reaching a book draw.

(b) It doesn't seem to matter where the bishop goes, but watch what happens when it goes to the wrong square: 1 Bd6? Rb2! 2 Be5 Rb5! 3 Bd4 Kg3! 4 Bxf2+ Kf3 5 Be1 Rb1 and the pinned bishop falls due to zugzwang.

(c) Rule out 1 Kxe2? Kg2 and the pawn queens.

153. A is the correct answer.
Choices: (a) Bd7 (b) Be6 (c) Bg2

(a) The next series of diagrams deal only with endings where the major pieces (queen and rook) make their debut if one side manages to queen a pawn.

It's well known that a rook pawn plus a bishop of the wrong color (one that doesn't control the queening square) cannot beat a lone king in front of the pawn. Since Black's immediate threat is Kg1, White must move his bishop, but where? The only decisive maneuver is 1 Bd7! Ke3 2 h4 Ke4 3 h5 Ke5 4 h6 Kf6 5 Be8! and Black is in zugzwang.

(b) Wrong is 1 Be6? Ke3 2 h4 Ke4 3 h5 Ke5 4 h6 Kf6 5 Bf5 (or 5 h7? Kg7 6 Bf5 Kh8) Kf7 7 Bh7 Kf6 8 Kd4 Kg5=.

(c) Black also gets back in time on 1 Bg2? Ke3! 2 h4 Kf4 3 Bf3 Ke5. The king cannot be dislodged after reaching h8.

154. A is the correct answer.
Choices: (a) h6 (b) Kb6 (c) Kb7

(a) The clincher is 1 h6! Bg8 2 Bb3! Bh7 3 Bc2+! Kxc2 4 d4 and one of the pawns will queen.

(b) Too slow is 1 Kb6? Kxd2 2 Kc5 Ke3 3 Kd6 Kf4 4 h6 Bg8 5 Ke7 Kg5=.

(c) No better is 1 Kb7? Kxd2.

155. C is the correct answer.
Choices: (a) a7 (b) Be2 (c) g4

(a) Premature is 1 a7? Bc6 2 Be2 e4!= (but not 2...Bxg2? 3 e4 shutting the bishop out).

(b) Black holds after 1 Be2? e4 2 dxe4 e5! closing the h1-a8 diagonal.

(c) White triumphs with 1 g4! Bc6 (if 1...e4 2 Bg2! exd3+ 3 Kd2!) 2 Bg2! Bxg2 3 e4 f5 4 gxf5 exf5 5 a7 fxe4 6 d4! (not 6 a8/Q? exd3 WITH CHECK and Bxa8) e3 7 dxe5 Kb5 8 e6 Kb6 9 e7 wins (the bishop is overburdened after 9...Bc6 10 a8/Q Bxa8 11 e8/Q).

156. A is the correct answer.
Choices: (a) Bd4 (b) Kg5 (c) Bb4

(a) Speed is of the essence: 1 Bd4! Be1! (otherwise Bxc3 draws) 2 Bxe3 Bd2 3 Bg5 Kf5 4 f4 Bxf4 5 Kh5! Bxg5 stalemate.

(b) Too slow is 1 Kg5? (losing a vital tempo) Kd5 2 Bb6 Bg1 3 Ba5 Kc4 guarding the pawn on c3 and wins.

(c) The stalemate defense is no longer an option after 1 Bb6? Kf5 2 Bd4 Be1 3 Bxe3 Bd7

157. B is the correct answer.
Choices: (a) Kf7 (b) Bf5+(c) Ke5

(a) Black trades all the pawns after 1 Kf7? Kxh4 2 Kxg7 Kg3 3 Be4 h4 4 Kf6 h3=.

(b) Black is forced to bury his own king by 1 Bf5+! Kxh4 2 Bh3 g5 (or 2...Kg5 3 Ke5 Kh6 4 Kf4 g5+ 5 Kg3 g4 6 Bxg4 hxg4 7 Kxg4 Kg6 8 g3! gaining the opposition) 3 Kf5 g4 4 Kf4! g3 (if 4...gxh3 5 g3 mate) 5 Kf3 Kg5 6 Kxg3 and the g-pawn will triumph after the h-pawn is captured.

(c) Stalemate beckons after 1 Ke5? Kxh4 2 Kf4=.

158. C is the correct answer.
Choices: (a) Kf5 (b) fxg4+ (c) g3

(a) Tempting but inadequate is 1 Kf5? g3! 2 gxh3 g2 3 Be3 Kh4=.

(b) White's hands are empty after 1 fxg4+? Kxg4 2 gxh3+ Kxh3=.

(c) White must safeguard the pawn that will deliver the final blow: 1 g3! h6 (if 1...gxf3 2 Kf5 and g4) 2 Be3 h2 3 Kf5 gxf3 4 Bf2! h1/Q 5 g4 mate!

159. A is the correct answer.
Choices: (a) d6 (b) Ka7 (c) Kb8

(a) Once again a profound knowledge of king and pawn endings is required to save White after 1 d6! Ke6 2 d7! Kxd7 3 Ka7! Be2 4 Kb8 Ba6 5 Ka7 Bc8 6 Kb8 Ba6 7 Ka7 Kxc7 8 Kxa6 Kd6 9 Kb5 Ke5 10 Kc4 Kf4 11 Kd3 Kxg4 12 Ke2 Kg3 13 Kf1 and the king gets back in time.

(b) White loses after 1 Ka7? Bc8 2 Kb8 Bxg4 3 d6 Ke5 4 c8/Q Bxc8 5 Kxc8 Kxd6.

(c) Equally bad is 1 Kb8? Ke5 2 c8/Q Bxc8 3 Kxc8 Kxd5 4 Kd7 Ke5 5 Ke7 Kf4, etc.

160. B is the correct answer.
Choices: (a) Ke1 (b) Bb3 (c) Kf2

(a) White can't win after 1 Ke1? d2+ 2 Ke2 Kb2 3 Bb3 Kc1 4 Kd3 d1/Q+ 5 Bxd1 Kxd1 6 Kc3 Ke2 7 Kb3 Kd3 8 Kxa3 Kc4 9 Ka4 Kc5=.

(b) A finesse is needed with 1 Bb3! Kb2 (if 1...Kd2 2 Kf2 Kc3 3 Ke1 d2+ 4 Ke2 wins) 2 Ke1 Kc1 3 Kf2! Kb2 (no better is 3...Kd2 4 Kf1 Ke3 5 Ke1 d2+ 6 Kd1 Kd3 7 Bg8! Kc3 8 Bf7 Kd3 9 Bb3 Kc3 10 Ke2) 4 Ke3 Kc3 5 Ke4! d2 (or 5...Kd2 6 Bc4) 6 Ke3 winning the pawn. (Note that the bishop is the "right color" to queen the a-pawn because it can control a8)

(c) Inadequate is 1 Kf2? d2 2 Ke3 (for 2 Ke2 Kb2 see "a") Kb2 3 Bb3 d1/Q! 4 Bxd1 Kxa2=.

161. A is the correct answer.
Choices: (a) Bc1 (b) Bf6 (c) Be5

(a) The only way to win is to beat a strategic retreat:: 1 Bc1! Kd3 2 Kb3 (not 2 Kxb4? Kc2=) Ke2 3 Kc2 Ke1 4 Bb2 Ke2 (or 4...b3+ 5 Kc3 Kd1 6 Ba3 Ke2 7 Bc1 Kd1 8 Kb2 wins) 5 Ba1! (not 5 Bd4? b3+ 6 Kc1 b2+ 7 Bxb2 Kd3=) e3 6 d3! Kf3 (if 6...Kf2 7 Bf6! e2 8 Bh4+ Ke3 9 Be1 b3+ 10 Kc3 b2 11 Bd2+ wins) 7 Bd4! Ke2 8 Bb2! Kf3 9 Bc1! and wins.

(b) Pointless is 1 Bf6? b3 2 Ka3 Kd3 3 Bg5 Kc2=.

(c) The bishop must leave this diagonal in view of 1 Be5? b3 2 Ka3 Kd3=.

162. A is the correct answer.
Choices: (a) g4+ (b) a7 (c) Ke3

(a) Black is forced to step on his own toes after 1 g4+! Bxg4 (or 1...Kxg4 2 a7) 2 Ke3! Bh3 3 Kf2! and the Bishop can't get on the long h1/a8 diagonal to stop the pawn. (See next diagram for a similar theme.)

(b) It's an easy draw after 1 a7? Bf3.

(c) Inadequate is 1 Ke3 Be8 2 a7 Bc6=.

163. C is the correct answer.
Choices: (a) Kb7 (b) Be6 (c) Be2

(a) The crude 1 Kb7? b5 is an immediate draw.

(b) White has no time for 1 Be6? Bf2 2 Bc4 b5! 3 Bxb5+ Ka5=.

(c) Black must be prevented from playing b5 at all cost: 1 Be2! Ka5 (or 1...Ka3 2 Bb5 Kxa2 3 Kb7 Kb3 4 Kxa7 Kb4 5 Kb7 Kxb5 6 a7 and queens) 2 Bf1! (premature is 2 Bb5? Ba3! 3 Kb7 Kxb5 4 Kxa7 Bd6! 5 Kb7 Bb8! 6 a4+ Ka5! 7 Kxb8 Kxa6=) Be3 3 Bb5! Kb4 4 a4! followed by Kc6-b7 wins.

164. B is the correct answer.
Choices: (a) Ba3 (b) Bh8 (c) h6

(a) White can't rush his king to the kingside fast enough after 1 Ba3? Bxd3 2 Kb2 e5! 3 Kc3 Be4! 4 Kd2 Kb7 5 Ke3 Bf5 6 Bb2 Kc6 7 Bxe5 Kd5 8 Kf4 Ke6 9 Bb2 Bc2 10 Kg5 Kf7=.

(b) The fastest way to get the king to g7 is 1 Bh8! Bxd3 2 Kb2 Kb7 (if 2...e5 3 Kc3! Bb1 4 Kc4 Kb7 5 Kd5 Kc7 6 Ke6 Kd8 7 Kf7 wins) 3 Kc3 Bf5 4 Kd4 Kc6 5 Ke5 Kd7 6 Kf6 Ke8 7 Kg7 (the reason for the strange first move is now clear) e5 8 h6 e4 9 h7 e3 10 Kh6! e2 11 Bc3 and wins.

(c) If 1 h6? Bxd3 draws because White won't get his king to h6 as in "b".

165. C is the correct answer.
Choices: (a) Ke8 (b) Bg8 (c) f5+

(a) Inaccurate is 1 Ke8? Be7 2 f5+ gxf5 3 Bxf5+ Kd6.

(b) No time for 1 Bg8? Bb4 2 Ke8 Ba5 3 Bxf7+ Kf5=.

(c) The crusher is 1 f5+! gxf5 (if 1...Kf6 2 Ke8 Be7 3 Bxg6! fxg6 4 fxg6 h4 5 g7 wins) 2 Bxf5+ Kf6 (if 2...Kxf5 3 Ke8 and the pawn queens) 3 Ke8 Be7 4 Bh3! h4 4 Bg4 h3 5 Bxh3 and Black is in zugzwang.

166. C is the correct answer.
Choices: (a) Kf5 (b) d8/Q (c) g4

(a) Opposite colored bishops are generally drawn if one side is a pawn or two ahead provided the weaker side can set up a blockade. Black has nothing to fear from 1 Kf5? Bf6 2 Bb3 Kd6 3 Ke4 Be7 and White can't penetrate.

(b) White can't break the blockade on dark squares after 1 d8/Q+ Kxd8 2 Kf7 Bf6 3 Bb3 Bg5 4 Kxg7 Ke7.

(c) White wins by freeing his h-pawn by 1 g4! hxg3 2 h4 Bf6 3 h5 g2 (or 3...Be5 4 d8/Q+ Kxd8 5 Kf7 Bf6 6 h6) 4 Bxg2 Kxe6 5 Bh3+ Ke7 6 h6 gxh6 7 d8/Q+ Kxd8 10 Kxf6, etc.

167. B is the correct answer.
Choices: (a) Ke5 (b) Kc3 (c) Kc5

(a) Going directly to win a piece fails: 1 Ke5? a5 2 Kf6 a4 3 Ke7 Kc8 (too hasty is 3...a4? 4 Kd7!) 4 Kf8 a4 5 g8/Q Bxg8 6 Kxg8 a3 7 Bxa3 Kxc7=.

(b) It's necessary to guard the c-pawn by shifting the bishop to a5, a task that requires delicate timing: 1 Kc3! Bf7 2 Kb4 Be6 3 Be5! Bf7 (or 3...Kc8 4 Kc5 Bb3 5 Kb5! Kb7 6 Kb4 Bf7 7 Kc5 Kc8 8 Kc6 Bg8 9 Bc3 as in the main line) 4 Kc5 Bb3 (if 4...a5 5 Kb5) 5 Kd6 Kc8 6 Bc3! Bg8 7 Ba5 Bf7 8 Ke7 Kb7 9

Kf8 followed by g8 winning a piece while the pawn on a5 is held at bay.

(c) An immediate draw is reached after 1 Kc5? a5! 2 Kb5 a4.

168. B is the correct answer.
Choices: (a) a4 (b) b4 (c) a3

(a) Fischer escaped with a draw after 1 a4? ("This natural push throws away the win!" — Fischer) Kc7 2 b4 Kb8 3 a5 Ka7 4 Kc4 Bg3 5 b5 Bf2 6 Be2 (if 6 Kd5 Be1 7 b6+ Ka6!; or 6 b6+ Bxb6 7 axb6+ Kxb6= "The theme underlying Black's defense is this: once he succeeds in sacrificing his bishop for both queenside pawns, then White will be left with the wrong bishop for his h-pawn" — Fischer) Be3 7 b6+ Kb7 8 Ka4 Kc6 9 Bb5+ Kc5 and White's pawns are stymied on 10 b7 Bf5 2 a6 Kb6=.

(b) "The Swiss endgame composer Fontana pointed out the proper method," wrote Fischer: 1 b4! Kc7 2 Ka5! Kb8 3 b5 Ba3 4 b6 Kc8 5 Ka6 Kb8 6 Bg2! and Black is in zugzwang. If 6...Kc8 (or 6...Bc5 7 a4) 7 Ka7 Bd4 8 a4, etc.

(c) On 1 a3 Be5 2 b4 Bb2 3 a4 Kc7 transposes into "a".

169. B is the correct answer.
Choices: (a) a7 (b) Ka7 (c) Kb8

(a) Rule out 1 a7? Nc6 followed by Nxa7 since it's impossible for a knight to mate a lone king.

(b) The subtle solution is 1 Ka7! Kb5 (or 1...Kc5 2 Nd4! Kxd4 3 Kb6) 2 Nb4! Ka5 3 Kb8 Nc6+ (or 3...Kxb4 4 Kc7 Ne6+ 5 Kb6 and the pawn queens) 4 Kc7 Na7 5 Kb7 and wins.

(c) Inadequate is 1 Kb8? Kb5 2 Nb4 Nc6+ 3 Kb7 (or 3 Nxc6 Kxa6!) Na5+ 4 Kc7 Nc6! 5 Kd6 Kb6=.

170. A is the correct answer.
Choices: (a) Ne5 (b) Ne3+ (c) Nf2

(a) White can draw with 1 Ne5! Bd3 (to stop Bf5+) 2 Bf5! (anyway) Bxf5 3 Nc4! b1/Q 4 Na3+ followed by Nxb1.

(b) 1 Ne3+? Kd2 ends any further discussion.

(c) The queen beats two uncoordinated minor pieces after 1 Nf2? Bd3 2 Nxd3 b1/Q.

171. B is the correct answer.
Choices: (a) Nc7+ (b) Nf6 (c) Nxd6

(a) The knight gets sadly misplaced after 1 Nc7+? Kb8 2 Na6+ Kc8 and Black wins! (Too cooperative is 2...Ka8? 3 Kc7! g3 4 Kc8 d5 5 h8/Q Bxh8 6 Nc7 mate.)

(b) White's must get his pawns moving fast even if it costs a piece: 1 Nf6! Bxf6 2 Kxd6 g3 3 e5 Bg7 (or 3...g2 4 exf6 g1/Q 5 h8/Q Kb7 6 Qg7+ Qxg7 7 fxg7 wins) 4 e6 g2 5 e7 g1/Q 6 e8/Q+ Kb7 7 Qc6+ Kb8 8 Qc7+ Ka8 9 Qc8 mate.

(c) It's only a draw after 1 Nxd6 g3 2 Nf7 Bg7 3 Ng5 g2 4 Nf3 b4 5 e5 g1/Q 6 Nxg1 Bxe5 7 Nf3 Bg7 8 Nd2 Kb8 9 Kb5.

172. C is the correct answer.
Choices: (a) a6 (b) Nc1 (c) Nxf4

(a) Too rash is 1 a6? Bd4 stopping the pawn once and for all.

(b) Tricky but unsound is 1 Nc1? Kxg2 (of course not 1...Bd4? 2 Ne2+) 2 Nb3 f3 3 a6 f2 4 a7 f1/Q 5 a8/Q+ Qf3 and Black's on top.

(c) The winning idea is similar to diagram 162: 1 Nxf4! Kxf4 (but not 1...Bd4? 2 Ne2+) 2 Kd3 Bh4 3 g3+! Bxg3 4 Ke2 Bh2 5 Kf1 and the bishop can't stop the pawn by getting to the critical g1-a7 diagonal.

173. A is the correct answer.
Choices: (a) Ne3 (b) Kc1 (c) Nf2

(a) Delicate timing is required to prevent stalemate. The only way to win is 1 Ne3! Ka2 (no better is 1...a2 2 Kc1 a3 3 Nc2 mate) 2 Nd5 Ka1 3 Nb4 a2 4 Kc1 a3 5 Nc2 mate.

(b) Rule out 1 Kc1? Ka2! (suicidal is 1...a2 2 Ne3 a3 3 Nc2 mate as in "a") 2 Kc2 (too late for 2 Ne3 Kb3) 2 Kc2 Ka1=.

(c) Black escapes after 1 Nf2? a2! (but not 1...Ka2? 2 Nd3! Ka1 3 Nb4 a2 4 Kc1 a3 5 Nf2 mate as in "a".

174. C is the correct answer.
Choices: (a) Nxg7 (b) Nxh6 (c) Ne3

(a) White's king can't approach without allowing stalemate after 1 Nxg7? Kxg7 2 Ke6 Kg8! 3 Kf6 Kf8 (holding the opposition) 4 g7+ Kg8=.

(b) A distinction without a difference is 1 Nxh6? gxh6 2 Kf6 Kg8 3 g7 Kh7=.

(c) The right way to snuff out stalemate is 1 Ne3 Kg8 2 Nd5 Kh8 3 Nf6! gxf6 4 Kf7 with mate in two.

175. B is the correct answer.
Choices: (a) Nd6 (b) d4 (c) Nxh6

(a) White can't win by 1 Nd6? Na7 2 d4 Kf4.

(b) White has to march his center pawn: 1 d4! Kf4 2 Ne7! (not 2 Nd6? Na7 3 Kg2 b5) Na7 3 Nc6! (gaining a vital tempo since now 3...Nxc6 4 d5 queens one of the pawns) Nc8 4 d5 Kf5 5 Ne7+ Nxe7 6 a7 and queens.

(c) Black is out of the woods after 1 Nxh6? Ke4.

176. C is the correct answer.
Choices: (a) Nf3 (b) Kb6 (c) Kc6

(a) The knight cannot wander freely because it is tethered to the pawn. Black holds by the skin of his teeth after 1 Nf3? Kb7! 2 a6+ Kb8 3 Kb6 Ka8 4 Nd4 h2 5 Nb5 h1/Q 6 Nc7+ Kb8 7 a7+ Kc8 8 a8/Q+ Qxa8 9 Nxa8=.

(b) The same defense works against 1 Kb6? Ka8 2 a6 Kb8 3 Ng4 Ka8 4 Nf6 h2 5 Ne8 h1/Q 6 Nc7+ Kb8 7 a7+ Kc8=.

(c) White gains a crucial tempo by triangulating with 1 Ka6! Ka8 2 Kb6 Kb8 3 a6 Ka8 4 Ng4! Kb8 5 a7+ Ka8 6 Nf6 h2 7 Ne8 h1/Q 8 Nc7 mate!

177. B is the correct answer.
Choices: (a) Kg7 (b) Nd4 (c) Nc3

(a) The natural approach permits a draw after 1 Kg7? Kc6 2 Nd4+ Kc5 3 Nb3+ Kc4 4 Nxa5+ Kb4 5 Nc6+ Kb3=.

(b) The only way to prevent a pawn swap is 1 Nd4! Kd6 2 Nb3! a4 3 Na1! Kd5 (if 3...Kc5 4 Kg7 Kb4 5 Kf6 a3 6 Nc2+ Kb3 7 bxa3! Kxc2 8 a4 wins) 4 Kg7 Kd4 5 Kf6 Kd3 6 Ke5 Kd2 7 Kd4 Kc1 8 Kc3 and wins.

(c) Too slow is 1 Nc3 Kc6 2 Kg7 Kc5 3 Kf6 Kb4 4 Ke5 Kb3 5 Nd1 Kc2=.

178. C is the correct answer.
Choices: (a) a5 (b) Kb4 (c) Kc4

(a) Hopeless is 1 a5? Kd5 2 a6 Kc6 3 a7 Kb7 4 Kd3 Ne5+ 5 Ke4 Nxg4 6 Kf5 h5 7 Kg5 Nf6! holding the precious pawn.

(b) Of no avail is 1 Kb4? Kd5 2 Kb5 Nd4+ 3 Kb6 Nb3 4 a5 Nxa5 5 Kxa5 Ke4 6 Kb4 Kf4 7 Kc3 Kxg4 8 Kd2 Kf3 9 Ke1 Kg2 and White's king can't get to the vital f1 square.

(c) The only defense is 1 Kc4! Ke5! 2 a5 Kd6 3 a6 Kc6 4 a7 Kb7 5 Kd5! Nh2 6 g5! hxg5 7 Ke4 Kxa7 8 Kf5 g4 9 Kf4 Kb6 10 Kg3=.

179. C is the correct answer.
Choices: (a) Nd5+ (b) Nd1+ (c) Kd1

(a) Hopeless is 1 Nd5+ Kf3 2 Kd2 h3 and this pawn can't be tackled on its way to a touchdown.

(b) Inadequate is 1 Nd1+? Kf3 2 Kd2 h3 3 Ke1 e3! (for 3...h2? 4 Nf2! see "c") 4 Kf1 e2+ and wins.

(c) Our old friend stalemate is the saving clause: 1 Kd1! h3 2 Ke1 h2 3 Nd1+ Kf3 4 Nf2 e3 5 Kf1! Kg3 (or 5...exf2=) 6 Nh1+ Kf3 7 Nf2 Kg3 8 Nh1+ Kh3 9 Ke2 Kg2 10 Kxe3 Kxh1 11 Kf2 walling Black in.

180. B is the correct answer.
Choices: (a) Kb4 (b) Kb2 (c) Kb3

(a) Rule out the brute force approach after 1 Kb4? Nd5+ and Nxc7.

(b) The winning concept involves distant opposition: 1 Kb2! Kxf3 (or 1...Kf4 2 Kc2 Ke5 3 Nc4+ Nxc4 4 c8/Q) 2 Kc1!! Kf4 3 Kc2 Kg5 (if 3...Ke5 4 Nc4+!) 4 Kd3 Kf6 5 Kd4 Ke6 6 Kc5 Na4+ 7 Kb6 Nc3+ 8 Ka6 and the pawn queens.

(c) White can't get to c5 via 1 Kb3? Kxf3 2 Kc2 Ke2! 3 Kc1 Ke1 (keeping the opposition) 4 Nc4 Nc8=.

181. C is the correct answer.
Choices: (a) h7 (b) Nc3+ (c) Kd5

(a) White can't win by 1 h7? a2 2 Nc3+ Ka3 3 Nxa2 Kxa2 4 Kd5 Kb3 5 Ke6 Kc4 6 Kf6 Kd5 7 Kg7 Ke6 8 Kxh8 Kf7 stalemate.

(b) Of no avail is 1 Nc3+? Ka5 2 Kc5 Nf7 3 h7 Nh8 4 Na2 Nf7 5 Kc4 Nh8 6 Kc4 Kb6 getting to the kingside.

(c) The king must get to the kingside pronto: 1 Kd5! Nf7 2 h7 a2 3 Nc3+ Kb3 4 Nxa2 Kxa2 5 h8/Q! (too hasty is 5 Ke6? Nxg5+ and Nxh7) Nxh8 6 Ke6 Kb3 7 Kf6 Kc4 8 Kg7 Kd5 9 Kxh8 Ke6 10 Kg7 Kf5 (or 10...Ke7 11 Kxg6 Kf8 12 Kh7) 11 Kh6 (a case of "trebuchet" — see introduction —whoever moves loses!) Ke6 12 Kxg6, etc.

182. A is the correct answer.
Choices: (a) Ne5 (b) Kxd8 (c) bxa4

(a) Mate looms after 1 Ne5! Nb7 (or 1...axb3 2 a3+) 2 Kc7 Nc5 (if 2...Na5 3 Nd3 mate; or 2...axb3 3 a3+ Kc5 4 Kxb7) 3 Nc6 mate.

(b) Black draws easily after 1 Kxd8 axb3.

(c) A try that fails is 1 bxa4? bxa4! 2 Nd6 a3! 3 b3 Kc3=.

183. B is the correct answer.
Choices: (a) Ba7 (b) Bg3 (c) Bh2

(a) A clever knight sacrifice saves the day after 1 Ba7? Ne5+ 2 Kc7 Nc6! 3 Kxc6 h2 4 b8/Q h1/Q with a book draw.

(b) The only correct post for the bishop is 1 Bg3! a2 (or 1...Kxg3 2 b8/Q+ Kg2 3 Qg8+ Kh1 4 Qxf7 a2 5 Qf1+ Kh2 6 Ke6) 2 b8/Q a1/Q 3 Qf4+ Ke2 4 Qe4+ Kd2 5 Bf4+ Kc3 6 Be5+ snaring the queen.

(c) Inaccurate is 1 Bh2? a2 2 b8/Q a1/Q 3 Qf4+ Ke2! 4 Qe4+ Kf2! (not possible with the bishop on g3 as in "b").

184. C is the correct answer.
Choices: (a) Bf5+ (b) Bd1 (c) Bc8

(a) Checking drives Black's king to a better place after 1 Bf5+?

Kf4 2 h4 Ng4+ 3 Ke6 (if 3 Bxg4 Kxg4=) Nh6 4 Be6 Kg3 5 h4 Kh4=.

(b) Black can establish a blockade on the dark squares after 1 Bd1? Nd7+ 2 Kg5 Ke5 3 h4 Nf6 4 Bc2 Ke6 5 Bf5+ Ke7 6 Kg6 Nh5! 7 Kxh5 Kf8 getting to h8.

(c) The superior bishop won by zugzwang: 1 Bc8! Kf4 (the king was on an unfortunate square since if 1...Nf3 2 Bb7+ and Bxf3 wins; or 1...Nd3 2 Bf5+ and Bxd3) 2 h4 Nf3 3 h5 Ng5 4 Bf5! (see diagram in introduction) Nf3 5 h6 Ng5 6 Kg6 Nf3 (zugzwang) 7 h7 Ne5+ 8 Kf6 and Black resigned.

185. B is the correct answer.
Choices: (a) Kf7 (b) Kf5 (c) Kf6

(a) An instant draw arises from 1 Kf7? Nc8! 2 a8/Q stalemate.

(b) The knight can only be dislodged by first capturing the pawn on c7: 1 Kf5! Ke7 (1...Kc8 2 Ke5 transposes into the main line) 2 Ke5 Kf7 3 Kd4 Ke6 4 Kc5 Ke7 5 Bf3 Kd7 6 Bg4+ Ke7 7 Kc6 Kd8 8 Kb7 Ke7 (zugzwang) 9 Kxc7 and wins.

(c) Another trap is 1 Kf6? Nc8! 2 a8/R stalemate.

186. A is the correct answer.
Choices: (a) Nb6 (b) Ne5 (c) Nd6

(a) A bishop and knight can force mate against a lone king in at most 34 moves. In certain cases (such as this) a win exists even if the weaker side has a minor piece: 1 Nb6! Be3 (or 1...Bd2 2 Nd5! Be1 3 Nf4 Bb4 4 Nd3 wins) 2 Na4! Bd2 3 Nc5! (not 3 Kxd2? Kb3) Bf4 3 Nd3 Bd2 4 Kxd2 with a garden variety book win.

(b) If 1 Ne5? Bf6! forces a piece swap. End of discussion.

(c) Black can free his king from the vice after 1 Nd6? Be7 2

Ne4 Bb4 3 Nf2 Ba3 4 Bd4 Bb2 because if 5 Bxb2 stalemates.

187. A is the correct answer.
Choices: (a) Bb1 (b) Bc2 (c) Bd3

(a) Black gets into zugzwang after 1 Bb1! Bg8 2 Ba2 a5 3 Bb3 a4 4 Ba2! (if 4 Bxa4 d4! frees the bishop) a3 5 Bb3 a2 6 Bxa2 d4 (zugzwang) 7 Bxg8 d3 8 Nf7 mate.

(b) Black wins the battle for a tempo and draws after 1 Bc2? Bg8 2 Bb3 a5 3 Ba2 a4=. Now White either has to retreat his knight or play Bb1 which allows d4.

(c) Going for a pawn is misguided: 1 Bd3? Bg8 2 Bxa6 d4 3 Bd3 Bd5=.

188. A is the correct answer.
Choices: (a) Bd7 (b) Bc6+ (c) Ke2

(a) The only defense is 1 Bd7! h2 (or 1...Nf3+ 2 Ke2 Nd4+ 3 Ke3 h2 4 Kxd4 h1/Q 5 Bc6+ and Bxh1) 2 Bc6+ Kg1 (again if 2...Nf3 3 Ke2 h1/Q 4 Bxf3+ draws) 3 Bh1! Kxh1 (Black must wall himself in; if 3...Ng2+ 4 Ke2 Kxh1 5 Kf1!=) 4 Kf2! and the knight can't budge the king from f1 and f2 (but not 4 Kf1? Nf3 5 Kf2 Nd2 6 Kg3 Kg1 wins).

(b) Natural moves are often fatal: 1 Bc6+? Kg1 (threatening Ng2) 2 Bh1 Kxh1 3 Kf1 Kh2 4 Kf2 Ng6 5 Kf1 Kg3 6 Kg1 Ne5 7 Kh1 Ng4 8 Kg1 h2+ 9 Kh1 Nf2 mate.

(c) White can't afford to lose a tempo by 1 Ke2? Kg1! 2 Bc6 Ng2 and the pawn can't be stopped.

189. B is the correct answer.
Choices: (a) Kxd7 (b) Nh6 (c) g6

(a) Black draws easily against 1 Kxd7? Kg4 2 Ke6 Kh5.

(b) Black's knight can't stop the pawn after 1 Nh6! Nc4+ 2 Kd5! (not 2 Kxd7? Kf4 3 g6 Ne5+ and Nxg6) Kf4 (or 2...Ne3+ 3 Ke5 Nc4+ 3 Kf6 wins) 3 g6 Nd6 4 Kxd6 (but not 4 g7? Ne8 5 g8/Q Nf6+ and Nxg8=) Kg5 6 g7 Kf6 7 Nf5! wins (instead of 6 g8/Q stalemate).

(c) Black can sacrifice his knight to stop the pawn after 1 g6 Nf5+ 2 Ke5 Kg4 3 Kf6 Kf4.

190. C is the correct answer.
Choices: (a) Kxg4 (b) Ne3 (c) Nh3

(a) Two knights are the only combination of two minor pieces that can't force mate against a lone king without pawns on the board. Ergo 1 Kxg4? Kg1 draws.

(b) Stalemate looms after 1 Ne3? Kg1 2 Ne2+ Kh1 3 Kf2 g3+ 4 Kf1 g2+ 5 Nxg2.

(c) If Black could get rid of his pawn, then it would be a book draw. But he gets mated after 1 Nh3! gxh3 2 Kf2 h2 (zugzwang) 3 Ng3.

191. A is the correct answer.
Choices: (a) Nf2 (b) Nf3+ (c) Kf4

(a) Theory states that two knights cannot beat a lone king plus a pawn which is at least three squares away from queening. However when one knight is able to blockade this pawn, a win usually can be found. When the pawn is two squares away from promoting, a win is possible only in exceptional cases such as this: 1 Nf2! Kh5 (if 1...Kg3 2 Nfg4 Kg2 3 Kf4 wins even faster) 2 Nfg4 Kh4 3 Kg6! Kg3 4 Kg5 Kg2 5 Kf4 Kh1 6 Kf3! Kg1 7 Kg3 Ka8 8 Nf3 h2 9 Nf2 mate.

(b) On 1 Nf3+ Kh5 2 Ng3+ Kh6=. Black either flees from the mating net or threatens ...h2 pitching the pawn to reach a book draw.

(c) A mistake is 1 Kf4? Kh5 2 Kf6 Kh6 reaching open space.

192. B is the correct answer.
Choices: (a) Bxg4 (b) Be4+ (c) Bd5

(a) White simply walks into a lost ending after 1 Bxg4? Nxg4 2 c7 Ba6. Black picks up the pawn and then forces mate with bishop and knight (unlike two knights, this dynamic duo can force mate against a lone king).

(b) Armed with the knowledge that two knights can't force mate, White hastens to swap bishops: 1 Be4+! Kg5 2 c7 Ba6 (or 2...Bd7 3 Bb7=) 3 c8/Q! Bxc8 4 Bb7! Bd7 (4...Bxb7 is stalemate) 5 Bc6! Be6! 6 Bd5! Bf5 7 Be4!=. Black either must swap or allow stalemate (7...Bxe4).

(c) No time for 1 Bd5? Ba6 2 c7 Bc8! 3 Bb7 Bxb7 4 c8/Q Nf3+ releasing the potential stalemate.

193. B is the correct answer.
Choices: (a) Nxf2+ (b) Nfg3+ (c) Neg3+

(a) Since two knights cannot force mate against a lone king 1 Nxf2+ Kg1 2 Nh3+ Kf1 3 Ne3+ Ke2 4 Nxg2 is drawn even if Black gives away his knight.

(b) After 1 Nfg3+! Kg1 2 Ng5! Black is in zugzwang and gets mated next depending on which knight moves (2...Nd3 3 Nh3 mate).

(c) Black slips out of the noose on 1 Neg3+? Kg1 2 Nd4 Nd3 3 Nde2+ Kf2.

194. B is the correct answer.
Choices: (a) Nb6 (b) Kh8 (c) N/4e5

(a) A crude attempt to make a new queen fails after 1 Nb6? Nb8! 2 Nxb8 Nd6 getting rid of the pesky pawn once and for all.

(b) A high-class waiting move puts Black in zugzwang: 1 Kh8! Ne7 (if 1...Kf8 2 Nb6 Nb8 3 Nxb8 Nd6 4 N/8d7+ and the pawn queens) 2 Nd6+ Kf8 3 Ne5! Nb8 5 Kh7! with mate next depending on which knight moves!

(c) Black draws easily on 1 N/4e5? Nd6 2 Nxd7 Nxb7!

195. B is the correct answer.
Choices: (a) Nc4 (b) Kc8 (c) Kc7

(a) Two knights can sometimes win if the pawn is not too far advanced and it can be blockaded. But Black must not be allowed to give up his pawn because 1 Nc4? d2! 2 Nxd2 Ka7 leads to a book draw.

(b) Put Black in zugzwang, then close in for the kill with both knights: 1 Kc8! Ka7 2 Kc7 Ka8 3 Nc4! d2 4 Nb6+ Ka7 5 Nc8+ Ka8 6 Nd7 d1/Q 7 Nb6 mate.

(c) White's plan is thwarted after 1 Kc7? Ka7 2 Kc6 Kb8.

196. C is the correct answer.
Choices: (a) f4 (b) Nf3 (c) Nd1

(a) A good try which only draws is 1 f4 Kxc3! (if 1...h2? 2 Nd1! Kxd4 3 Nf2) 2 Nf3 b5 3 f5 b4+ 4 Ka2 Kc2 5 Nd4+ Kc3 6 Nf3 Kc2=.

(b) 1 Nf3 Kxc3 2 g4 b5 3 g5 b4+ 4 Ka2 Kc2 5 Nd4+ draws as in "a".

(c) White gains a crucial tempo by giving up the knight on d4 instead of the one on c3: 1 Nd1! h2 2 f4 Kxd4 3 Nf2 Kc3 (if 3...Ke3 4 Ng4+ and Nxh2) 4 f5 b5 5 f6 b4+ 6 Ka2 Kc2 7 f7 b3+ 8 Ka3 b2 9 f8/Q b1/Q 10 Qf5+ Kc1 11 Qf4+ Kc2 12 Qe4+! Kc1 13 Qe3+ Kc2 14 Qd3+ Kc1 15 Qd1 mate.

197. C is the correct answer.
Choices: (a) Bd8 (b) Nc3 (c) Nd2

(a) The pawn can't be stopped from queening on 1 Bd8? Kc5.

(b) Also wrong is 1 Nc3? Kd3 (but not 1...g1/Q+ 2 Ne2+ and Nxg1).

(c) Stalemate again comes to the rescue after 1 Nd2! Bd5 (if 1...g1/Q 2 Nf3+) 2 Bd8 Kc5 3 Nb3+! Bxb3 4 Bg5! g1/Q (or 5...Kd4 6 Bd8 Kc5 7 Bg5=) 5 Be3+ Qxe3=.

198. B is the correct answer.
Choices: (a) Be6+ (b) Ba6+ (c) Ne6

(a) Some moves work only against bad defense, such as 1 Be6+? Kb8! (of course not 1...Kd8? 2 Bd7! e5 3 Kd6 h1/Q 4 Ne6 mate) 2 Nd7+ Ka7! (again not 2...Ka8 3 Kb6 h1/Q 4 Bd5 mate) and White runs out of checks.

(b) The reason for White's pawn is twofold: it stops Black from queening with check and is needed when the storm is over: 1 Ba6+! Kd8 (too cooperative is 1...Kb8? 2 Kb6 h1/Q 3 Nd7+ Ka8 4 Bb7 mate) 2 Ne6+ Ke8 3 Be2! h1/Q (not 2...Kf7? 3 Bf3) 4 Bh5+! Qxh5 5 Ng7+ Kf7 6 Nxh5 Ke6 7 Ng3 Ke5 8 Kd7 e6 9 Ke7 Kf4 10 Kxe6 Kxg3 11 e5 and the last pawn standing is decisive.

(c) A careless transposition of moves loses after 1 Ne6? h1/Q 2 Ba6+ Kb8 3 Nc5 Ka7 and it's just a matter of time before the queen prevails against two minor pieces.

199. C is the correct answer.
Choices: (a) Nxe4 (b) Bd1 (c) Nd5

(a) A poisonous temptation is 1 Nxe4? c2 2 Nd2 Ka4! and Black wins (but not 2...c1/Q+ 3 Nc4+ Ka4 4 Bd1+ Qxd1 5 Nb2+ and Nxd1 as in "c".

(b) Trying to halt the pawns is futile: 1 Bd1?+ e3 2 Nd5 e2 3 Bxe2 c2 4 Ne3 c1/Q+ 5 Nc4+ Ka6! and wins (but not 5...Ka4

6 Bd1+! as in "c").

(c) White's last pawn does wonders after 1 Nd5! c2 2 Ne3 c1/Q+ 3 Nc4+ Ka4 (if 3...Ka6 4 Bc8 mate) 4 Bd1+! Qxd1 5 Nb2+ Ka3 6 Nxd1, etc.

200. A is the correct answer.
Choices: (a) Nc1 (b) Bf7 (c) Nd4

(a) White can't stop the pawn from queening but can create enough threats to neuter the queen after 1 Nc1! h2 2 Be8+ Ka5 (if 2...Kb4 3 Nd3+ Kc4 4 Nf2 stops the pawn cold) 3 Nd3 h1Q 4 b4+ Kb6 5 Nb2! a5 (or 5...Qa1 6 Na4+ Qxa4 7 Bxa4 wins) 6 Na4+ Ka6 7 b5 mate!

(b) White stops the pawn temporarily but the cost is too great: 1 Bf7? Kxb3 2 Bxd5+ Kxb2 3 Kc7 a5, etc.

(c) White is powerless after 1 Nd4? h2 2 Kb7 h1/Q 3 Bc2+ Kb4!

INDEX OF PLAYERS AND COMPOSERS

INDEX OF PLAYERS AND COMPOSERS

(numbers refer to diagrams)